CURRICULUM CENTER

Reading STREET

Grades 3-6

Scott Foresman

ELL and Transition Handbook

PEARSON
Scott Foresman

Editorial Offices: Glenview, Illinois • Parsippany, New Jersey • New York, New York
Sales Offices: Boston, Massachusetts • Duluth, Georgia • Glenview, Illinois
Coppell, Texas • Sacramento, California • Mesa, Arizona

D1472411

ISBN: 0-328-14556-4

4 5 6 7 8 9 10 V031 14 13 12 11 10 09 08 07

Contents

Overview: Support for English Language Learners

This **ELL and Transition Handbook** provides practical tips and professional development for teachers who are supporting the literacy development of English language learners. The instructional strategies for English language learners that are embedded in *Scott Foresman Reading Street* are explained in detail in this Handbook. Additional articles and lessons will help teachers customize support for English language learners in reading, writing, listening, and speaking at all levels of English proficiency.

ELL How to Use the ELL and Transition Handbook

Introduction Refresh your awareness of English language learners in the United States by reading this brief article.

Part One: English Language Learning and Literacy Expand your repertoire of successful strategies for developing English literacy skills in children at all levels of English proficiency.

Lay the groundwork by reading:

- Jim Cummins on the Three Pillars of English language learning
- Georgia Earnest García on best practices for literacy
- Lily Wong Fillmore on preparing English learners for assessment

Learn effective strategies through these research-based articles and accompanying reproducible teaching and assessment tools:

- Welcoming Newcomers
- Sheltering Instruction
- What Reading Teachers Should Know About Language
- Vocabulary Strategies
- Effective Writing Instruction
- Cultural Affirmation and Family Involvement
- Helping the Helpers (aides, tutors, and classroom volunteers)
- English Language Learners and Assessment

Part Two: Grammar Instruction for English Language Learners Choose lessons and practice pages from this section to supplement regular grammar instruction. These Grammar Transition Lessons and Practice Pages, designed especially for English language learners, will help students "unlock" the English language, build sentences, and use nouns, verbs, pronouns, adjectives, adverbs, prepositions, and conjunctions correctly, extending their language knowledge.

Part Three: Phonics Instruction for English Language Learners Address students' needs by teaching or reinforcing print awareness and alphabet skills, and tackle the challenging letter-sound correspondences that pose difficulties for English language learners. Choose the appropriate Phonics Transition Lessons and Practice Pages to provide instruction on consonant sounds and blends, varying English vowel sounds, and other phonics challenges. Teach word study skills involving word endings, contractions, prefixes, suffixes, Greek and Latin roots, cognates, and other vocabulary builders.

Professional Resources and the **Index** are helpful reference tools.

Introduction:
English Language Learners

Teachers and schools across the United States are welcoming increasing numbers of English language learners (ELLs) into their classrooms. English learners make up the fastest growing K–12 student population in the United States. Since the 1989–1990 school year, the population of English learners in U.S. public schools has nearly doubled (Padolsky, 2005). The current enrollment of English language learners is about 5.5 million, and it is expected that this student population will continue to grow over the next several decades (Collier and Thomas, 2002; Leos, 2004).

While Spanish is the home language of the greatest number of English learners in U.S. schools, more than 400 different languages are spoken in schools across the country (Kindler, 2002). Most states have experienced an influx of ELL enrollment. The states with the largest student populations of English learners include California, Texas, New York, Florida, Illinois, and Arizona (Padolsky, 2005). Nearly every educator in all fifty states has become more aware of the needs of English learners.

In the current legislative climate, English language learners are expected to participate in yearly high-stakes tests. Research has consistently shown that ELL children usually require at least five years, on average, to catch up to native-speaker norms in academic language proficiency (Cummins, 1981). Nevertheless, many English learners must take the tests whether or not they have developed academic language proficiency in English.

While English language learners share many characteristics with other students, they need types of support and scaffolding that are specific to them. They represent a highly diverse population. They come from many home language backgrounds and cultures. They have a wide range of prior educational and literacy experiences in their home languages. They come to school with varying levels of English language proficiency and experience with mainstream U.S. culture.

Teachers need support to identify and respond appropriately to the varying needs of English learners in their classrooms. They need to know how to help these students develop fluency as readers, writers, listeners, and speakers of academic English at the same time that the students are required to learn grade-level content-area concepts. Yet many teachers have not had opportunities to receive specialized training. They feel unprepared to help English learners excel.

This Handbook is designed to help teachers, whether they have one English learner in the classroom or many. It offers strategies and activities to help teachers scaffold and support their instruction so that all English learners can learn in ways that are comprehensible and meaningful, and in ways that promote the academic success and achievement of all students.

References

Collier, V., and W. Thomas, 2002. *A National Study of School Effectiveness for Language Minority Students' Long-Term Academic Achievement.* Santa Cruz, CA and Washington, DC: Center for Research on Education, Diversity & Excellence. http://www.crede.org/research/llaa/1.1_es.html

Cummins, J., 1981. The Role of Primary Language Development in Promoting Educational Success for Language Minority Students. In *Schooling and Language Minority Students: A Theoretical Framework.* Sacramento, CA: California Department of Education.

Kindler, A. L., 2002. *Survey of the States' Limited English Proficient Students and Available Programs and Services: 2001–2002 Summary Report.* Washington, DC: U.S. Office of English Language Acquisition.

Leos, K., 2004. *No Child Left Behind.* Paper presented at the annual conference of the National Association for Bilingual Education, Albuquerque, New Mexico.

National Center for Education Statistics, 2002. *Public Elementary/Secondary School Universe Survey 2001–2002* and *Local Education Agency Universe Survey 2001–2002.* Washington, DC: U.S. Department of Education Institute for Education Sciences.

Padolsky, D., 2005. *How Many School-Aged English Language Learners (ELLs) Are There in the U.S.?* Washington, DC: National Clearinghouse for English Language Acquisition (NCELA). http://www.ncela.gwu.edu/expert/faq/01leps.html

Part 1
English Language Learning and Literacy

Contents

The Three Pillars of English Language Learning

Dr. Jim Cummins, the University of Toronto

In order to understand how English learners develop second-language literacy and reading comprehension, we must distinguish between three different aspects of language proficiency:

Conversational fluency This dimension of proficiency represents the ability to carry on a conversation in face-to-face situations. Most native speakers of English have developed conversational fluency by age 5. This fluency involves use of high-frequency words and simple grammatical constructions. English learners generally develop fluency in conversational English within a year or two of intensive exposure to the language in school or in their neighborhood environments.

Discrete language skills These skills reflect specific phonological, literacy, and grammatical knowledge that students can acquire in two ways—through direct instruction and through immersion in a literacy-rich and language-rich environment in home or in school. The discrete language skills acquired early include:

- knowledge of the letters of the alphabet
- knowledge of the sounds represented by individual letters and combinations of letters
- the ability to decode written words

Children can learn these specific language skills concurrently with their development of basic English vocabulary and conversational fluency.

Academic language proficiency This dimension of proficiency includes knowledge of the less frequent vocabulary of English as well as the ability to interpret and produce increasingly complex written language. As students progress through the grades, they encounter:

- far more low-frequency words, primarily from Greek and Latin sources

- complex syntax (for example, sentences in passive voice)
- abstract expressions

Acquiring academic language is challenging. Schools spend at least 12 years trying to teach all students the complex language associated with academic success. It is hardly surprising that research has repeatedly shown that English language learners, on average, require *at least* 5 years of exposure to academic English to catch up to native-speaker norms.

Effective instruction for English language learners is built on three fundamental pillars.

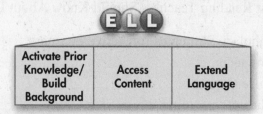

Activate Prior Knowledge/ Build Background

No learner is a blank slate. Each person's prior experience provides the foundation for interpreting new information. In reading, we construct meaning by bringing our prior knowledge of language and of the world to the text. The more we already know about the topic in the text, the more of the text we can understand. Our prior knowledge enables us to make inferences about the meaning of words and expressions that we may not have come across before. Furthermore, the more of the text we understand, the more new knowledge we can acquire. This expands our knowledge base (what cognitive psychologists call *schemata,* or underlying patterns of concepts). Such comprehension, in turn, enables us to understand even more concepts and vocabulary.

It is important to *activate* students' prior knowledge because students may not realize what they know about a particular topic or issue. Their knowledge may not facilitate learning unless that knowledge is brought to consciousness.

Teachers can use a variety of strategies to activate students' prior knowledge:	
Brainstorming/Discussion	Visual stimuli
Direct experience	Student writing
Dramatization	Drawing

When students don't already have knowledge about a topic, it is important to help them acquire that knowledge. For example, in order to comprehend texts such as *The Midnight Ride of Paul Revere,* students need to have background knowledge about the origin of the United States.

Access Content

How can teachers make complex academic English comprehensible for students who are still in the process of learning English?

We can *scaffold* students' learning by modifying the input itself. Here are a variety of ways of modifying the presentation of academic content to students so that they can more effectively gain access to the meaning.

Using Visuals Visuals enable students to "see" the basic concepts we are trying to teach much more effectively than if we rely only on words. Among the visuals we can use are:

• *pictures/diagrams*   • *vocabulary cards*
• *real objects*   • *graphic organizers*   • *maps*

Dramatization/Acting Out For beginning English learners, *Total Physical Response*, in which they follow commands such as "Turn around," can be highly effective. The meanings of words can be demonstrated through *gestures* and *pantomime.*

Language Clarification This category of teaching methods includes language-oriented activities that clarify the meaning of new words and concepts. *Use of dictionaries*, either bilingual or English-only, is still the most direct method of getting access to meaning.

Making Personal and Cultural Connections We should constantly search for ways to link academic content with what students already know or what is familiar to them from their family or cultural experiences. This not only validates children's sense of identity, but it also makes the learning more meaningful.

Extend Language

A systematic exploration of language is essential if students are to develop a curiosity about language and deepen their understanding of how words work. Students should become *language detectives* who investigate the mysteries of language and how it has been used throughout history to shape and change society.

Students also can explore the building blocks of language. A large percentage of the less frequently heard academic vocabulary of English derives from Latin and Greek roots. Word formation follows predictable patterns. These patterns are very similar in English and Spanish.

When students know rules or conventions of how words are formed, it gives them an edge in extending vocabulary. It helps them figure out the meanings of words and how to form different parts of speech from words. The exploration of language can focus on meaning, form, or use:

Focus on meaning Categories that can be explored within a focus on meaning include:

• *home language equivalents or cognates*
• *synonyms, antonyms, and homonyms*
• *meanings of prefixes, roots, and suffixes*

Focus on form Categories that can be explored within a focus on form include:

• *word families*   • *grammatical patterns*
• *words with same prefixes, roots, or suffixes*

Focus on use Categories that can be explored within a focus on use include:

• *general uses*   • *idioms*
• *metaphorical use*   • *proverbs*
• *advertisements*   • *puns and jokes*

The Three Pillars

• Activate Prior Knowledge/ Build Background
• Access Content
• Extend Language

establish a solid structure for the effective instruction of English language learners.

English Language Learners and Literacy: Best Practices

Dr. Georgia Earnest García, the University of Illinois at Urbana-Champaign

Like other children, English language learners come to school with much oral language knowledge and experience. Their  knowledge and experience in languages other than English provide skills and world knowledge that teachers can build on.

Making literacy instruction comprehensible to English language learners is essential. Many of the teaching strategies developed for children who are proficient in English can be adapted for English learners, and many strategies from an English as a Second Language curriculum also are useful in "mainstream" reading education.

Building on Children's Knowledge

It is vital to learn about each student's literacy development and proficiency in the home language. School personnel should ask parents:

- How many years of school instruction has the child received in the home language?
- Can the child read and write in that language?
- Can the child read in any other language?

Students can transfer aspects of home-language literacy to their English literacy development, such as phonological awareness and reading (or listening) comprehension strategies. If they already know key concepts and vocabulary in their home languages, then they can transfer that knowledge to English.

A teacher need not speak each student's home language to encourage English language learners to work together and benefit from one another's knowledge. Students can communicate in their home languages and English, building the content knowledge, confidence, and English skills that they need to participate fully in learning.

Devising activities in which students who share home languages can work together also allows a school to pool resources, such as bilingual dictionaries and other books, as well as home-language tutors or aides. A goal of home-language support is to help students who have skills in a first language to access this knowledge and use it to improve both their literacy and their knowledge in English.

Sheltering Instruction in English

Often, beginning English language learners may not understand what their classroom teachers say or read aloud in English. These students benefit when teachers shelter, or make comprehensible, their literacy instruction.

Sheltered instructional techniques include using:

- consistent, simplified, clearly enunciated, and slower-paced oral language to explain literacy concepts or activities
- gestures, photos, illustrations, drawings, real objects, dramatization, and/or physical action to illustrate important concepts and vocabulary
- activities that integrate reading, writing, listening, and speaking, so students see, hear, read, and write new vocabulary, sentence structures, and content

When it is clear from students' actions and responses that they understand what is being said, teachers can vary their strategies. As students' comprehension expands, teachers can gradually curtail their use of adapted oral language and of gestures, illustrations, and dramatizations.

Adapting Literacy Activities

Teachers can use many instructional activities developed for native English speakers with English language learners. For example, teacher read-alouds, shared reading, and paired reading can allow an English learner to follow the text during a reading. Such techniques improve students' learning skills and comprehension.

Similarly, interactive journal writing, in which the teacher and student take turns writing entries, allows students to explore topics and ask questions. It also allows teachers to engage in ongoing authentic assessment of student proficiency and to pinpoint areas of misunderstanding.

Small group instruction and discussion also are helpful. Beginning English learners benefit from the repeated readings of predictable texts with illustrations, especially when the teacher has provided a brief preview of each text to introduce the topic of the story and new vocabulary.

Repeated reading aloud of such texts provides English language learners with multiple opportunities to match the text they read with the words they hear. When students participate in shared reading and echo the spoken text or read the words aloud chorally, anxiety about pronunciation or decoding errors is reduced. When teachers choose texts that are culturally familiar and ask English learners personal questions related to the text, the result is a lower-risk learning environment and an increased opportunity for students to make accurate inferences.

It is important for teachers to realize that beginning English language learners often do not recognize the meanings of English words as they decode them. Many words that typically are included in beginning reading instruction for native English speakers may not be part of the oral vocabulary of English language learners. For this reason, decoding instruction must be combined with vocabulary and comprehension instruction so that English language learners understand the goal of reading—comprehension.

Examples of Teaching Strategies

Before students read, use graphic organizers to map a concept from the selection. Let students brainstorm in pairs or small groups for words that are related to the concept. Then introduce other related words, including vocabulary from the reading. When possible, illustrate new concepts or vocabulary with drawings or photographs of the items. The graphic organizer will help orient students to the setting or context of the reading. Students will thus be familiar with the selection's subject before they begin to read.

Semantic Mapping Working with graphic organizers can help teach vocabulary and concepts in subject areas. Students may fill in their own maps or help the teacher to do so by dictating the words to enter into the map. For example, students might benefit by mapping the names of different forms of writing. Ask students to meet in small groups to discuss examples of each kind of writing that they know about. Have them list the names in their home language, and then you can write the English names beneath. Then ask students to enter the words into a vocabulary notebook.

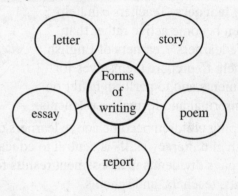

Examples of Writing After Reading

Summarizing Students can write and illustrate short summaries about what they have learned that day to help them review new vocabulary and reinforce content learning. They can keep these in a folder or take them home to their families to show their progress. Post key words on the board or provide a sentence frame to get students started.

Dialogue Journals In a dialogue journal, students write short entries addressed to the teacher. The teacher replies with answers to questions, modeling correct English usage in the feedback. The dialogue journal can also serve as an informal assessment tool.

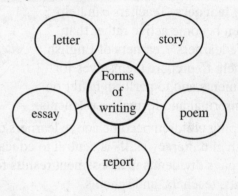

Preparing English Language Learners for Assessment

Dr. Lily Wong Fillmore, the University of California, Berkeley

Assessment is a vital part of reading education for all children.

- **diagnostic evaluations**
- **ongoing assessments during instruction**
- **tests that measure children's learning and the effectiveness of teaching**

How well do assessment techniques and instruments meet the needs of English language learners? "High-stakes" reading and content area tests, such as state tests, typically are designed and normed for proficient English speakers. How well do these assessments accommodate the developing proficiency of English learners?

Teachers look for strategies to help English learners prepare for—and perform well on—assessments, so that evaluations will reflect children's learning and inform instruction.

Active learners Teachers can help children become active rather than passive learners. Learners of English need help to prepare themselves for assessments and to perform better on both informal and formal assessments.

Helping children become active learners of English and literacy skills is central to education, and it pays dividends in assessment results for students, teachers, and schools.

Academic English How proficient must English learners become to demonstrate their mastery of language arts and reading—in English tests and other assessments? These students would need to be fully proficient in English to match the test results of their native-English-speaking peers. Yet teachers cannot declare the assessment of English language learners to be "mission impossible." Helping children improve their understanding and use of academic English is an essential way to prepare them for assessment. Here are a few strategies a teacher can use.

- Engage children in instructional conversations about reading selections and other content as often as possible, helping them hear academic English from both teacher and classmates. Find ways for the English learners to use the language as much as possible, but also recognize that children who are included in learning can achieve better grasp of English even when they are not producing polished responses.

- Draw children's attention to the features of academic language in reading selections and text materials. Help them understand it through various methods, such as these:

discussing text content in language that English learners can access more easily—that is, simpler English or, if possible, their home languages
using pictures, demonstrations, and gestures to enhance access to meaning
providing ample grade-level-appropriate discussion of content, including supportive explanations and questions for all students

Native English speakers and English learners together can learn academic language.

- Recognize that it takes years for children to master academic English, but help them make progress every step of the way.

- Teach the language used in tests and other assessments.

Assessment language The practice of "teaching to the test" is often criticized. Limiting one's teaching only to the skills and topics that figure in testing inhibits children's 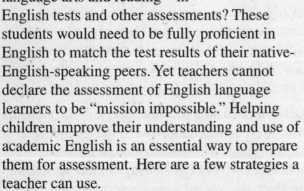 English learning. But helping children understand the language of tests and other assessment instruments not only helps level the playing field, but also allows children to learn more English and accurately show what they learn.

- Call children's attention to words, phrases, and constructions that often figure in test items. Words such as *both* and *not* may seem simple, but their uses in test questions prove otherwise. Help English learners understand such words and how they frame ideas.

- Teach children the logic of test questions. Use real test items or models of test items offered at many states' departments of education (or districts') Web sites. Show children, for one example, that the question "Which of the following is NOT a sentence?" entails that all of the listed choices except one <u>are</u> sentences.
- Teach children to read carefully. Native English speakers may occasionally benefit by reading test questions and then skimming test passages for answer information, but this tactic does not serve English learners well. They need to read and understand the words, ideas, and directions.

Using the Three Pillars

Think of preparing children for assessment in terms of the Three Pillars of English language learning.

- Comprehension of texts requires the **activation of prior knowledge.** English learners, like all children, have such knowledge, but they need help to see that what they know can be relevant to the text. They should bring their knowledge to bear in order to understand what they read. They also need help to use materials they read in order to **build background knowledge** for learning. Teachers support children in activating prior knowledge and building background for tests by discussing the meanings of texts and by relating what children know to new materials and ideas.
- English learners need help in **accessing the content** of texts that are presented in the language that they are learning. Teachers provide access by teaching children strategies for using context to understand and interpret texts. Examples of these strategies include:

reading texts to students, with ample discussion of meaning if students cannot yet read the texts by themselves, at least on the first go-around
guiding students to assume that the text should make sense and that meaning can be determined by figuring out what the words, phrases, and sentences mean

asking questions about meaning as it unfolds in the text
helping children recognize that some parts of many texts provide background knowledge while other parts reveal the main messages
teaching how to relate new information presented in a text to what is already known
training students to make inferences about meaning, based on the words and phrases in a text

- The texts that are read to children or that they read give them reliable access to academic English, provided that teachers call attention to the language. Teachers then can support the **extension of language** by methods such as these:

identifying interesting—not just new—phrases and commenting on them, inviting children to try using them, and providing scaffolds as needed
modeling the uses of language from texts in other activities
encouraging children to remember and keep records of words they learn from texts
reminding them when words and phrases encountered earlier show up again in different contexts

Teachers are overwhelmed by testing for accountability, but the most important testing is informal assessment that reveals how well students are learning what they need to learn; whether they understand what they read; and whether instructional activities are effective. Such assessment need not be elaborate. Monitoring participation levels can reveal who understands the materials. Asking children what they think is happening in a text reveals their comprehension. Asking children what they think words or phrases mean can show whether they are trying to make sense of text.

With the help of teachers—and their own engagement in comprehension—English learners can prepare for and improve their performance in informal and formal assessments.

Welcoming Newcomers to the Mainstream Classroom

Students who are new to the United States or to English-language instruction are among the most challenging and rewarding students to teach.

Newcomers offer great potential to enrich the classroom experience of all students. They can share a wealth of experience and prior knowledge with their classmates.

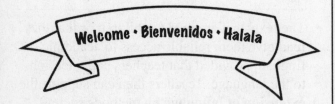

Welcome · Bienvenidos · Halala

Newcomers' levels of educational experience vary widely. Some may be fluent in conversational English and other languages and will be familiar with school environments. Others may never have attended school before. Some will be highly literate in their home languages, and some may have minimal or no literacy skills.

The teacher's first concern must be to help each child learn the basic concepts and vocabulary needed to participate in school life.

Prepare

Learn as much as possible about your newcomer students in order to tailor instruction to their individual needs. Consider drawing up a checklist:

Name_____

Home language? _____

Reads in home language? __Yes__No

Writes in home language? __Yes__No

Do family members read? __Yes__No

Is child read to at home? __Yes__No

Family can help with homework?__Yes__No

Find out from parents or other sources about educational practices in the student's home country or culture. For example, if the student is accustomed to memorizing and reciting material in a group, he or she may feel anxious about independent work or homework, particularly if the family is not able to help the child in English.

Newcomers who are acquiring English may experience identifiable stages of adjustment and adaptation.

- **A Silent Period** For a child quite new to an English-language environment, a "silent period" is normal. During this period, students chiefly watch and listen. The child may be learning classroom routine and acquiring basic vocabulary by watching and listening. Recognize that the child is learning even though he or she may not yet be speaking in class. After a time, students will gain confidence and begin to join in class activities.

- **Culture Shock** The abrupt severing of ties to anything familiar can cause newcomer students to experience stresses that may affect schoolwork. As part of the process of working through such stresses, some children may enter a short regression phase. In this phase, newcomers may prefer to spend much of their time with family or friends from the home culture and to temporarily reject the new language and culture. Help students to cope with this phase by providing extra help and attention when possible. A bilingual friend or classroom aide can help to make the environment feel more navigable to the child and can help to alleviate any feelings of anxiety or sadness.

Getting Started in the Classroom

The first days in a new classroom are important to students and their families. Before classes begin, you may wish to plan a small reception for newcomers. Invite the students' parents or other family members, and include someone who can translate. The presence of family can lessen an English learner's nervousness and introduce family members to you and to the school environment and resources.

- **Orient the newcomer to the classroom.** Have students help you to label the classroom and the objects in it with sticky notes. Pronounce the name of each item as you do, and use the word in a short sentence. *"Desk. This is your desk."*

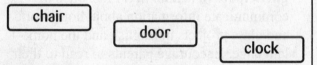

- **Demonstrate crucial skills.** Provide students with a map of the school building, with their classrooms clearly labeled. Post a seating chart where newcomers can easily see it, so that they can learn classmates' names. Go through the assigned textbooks, and help students understand what content area is covered in each book.

- **Show interest in and respect for each student's home culture.** Create opportunities for the class to learn more about the newcomer's home country and culture. Learn a few phrases in the child's home language. A cheerful greeting that includes the child's name can be used to help make the child feel welcome. Make a special effort to learn the correct pronunciation of the child's name.

- **Provide a "buddy."** A buddy system in the first weeks or months can help children navigate a new physical and social environment in ways that help them feel more secure. The buddy need not speak the same home language as the English language learner, though a buddy who does speak the same language might enable him or her to function as a peer tutor.

- **Try to provide a risk-free learning environment.** Anxiety about academic performance, especially about speaking in front of the class, can interfere significantly with a student's ability to learn. Create opportunities for students to practice speaking English without worrying about errors they may make. Accept errors in speech without comment, and model the correct phrasing.

- **Include newcomers in classroom routines.** Assign newcomers their share of regular classroom chores. Such responsibilities can help them feel they are part of the group. Students can be shown how to successfully carry out routine tasks without using or needing extensive English. Such activities, especially when performed with English-speaking partners, also can teach useful everyday vocabulary.

Teaching Strategies

Educational strategies should assist students to learn in content areas at the same time that they acquire the new language. Many commonly used teaching strategies can be adapted for English language learners. Remember that students' skills in the home language can be transferred to English learning. For this reason, encourage students to continue to speak and read in the home language. If possible, obtain the help of an English speaker who also speaks the student's home language and who can work with students to clarify key concepts.

- **Build on students' prior knowledge.**
Newcomers often have knowledge bases that
are much greater than their skill levels in
English. Find ways to gauge students'
familiarity with the topics of upcoming
lessons. Regularly using visual aids, such as
semantic maps, K-W-L charts, or time lines,
can help you determine how much each child
already knows or needs to learn about a topic.
If you show a student a diagram of the Earth,
Sun, and Moon, for example, and ask for
words that the student can associate with the
image, you can get information about how
much the child has learned about the Solar
System.

Know	Want to know	Learned

- **Encourage students to use learning
resources.** Teach students how to use a
children's dictionary, and encourage them to
use it frequently to find the words they need.
(Beginning English learners might use a
picture dictionary.) Ask them to start their own
word banks by listing frequently used
vocabulary in a notebook. You may wish to
allow newcomers to keep their word banks in a
computer file, which would make adding new
words and alphabetizing easier. Make sure
students know where the library or media
center is and how to use it. If possible, provide
a bilingual dictionary in the classroom for
students' use.

- **Use environmental print to teach.** Put up
posters and other materials from periodicals
and magazines. If possible, provide students
with parallel texts about the same topic in
English and in the home language. Such
materials can help children make connections
between their prior knowledge in the home
language and their new English vocabulary.

- **Invite the families of newcomers to
participate in school life.** Find ways to
communicate information about homework
and class projects in English and the home
language. Encourage parents to read to their
children in the home language and, if possible,
to share stories in English. Make them aware
that literacy skills in the home language can
help students transfer those skills to English.
You might suggest titles of engaging children's
books in English or the home language that can
provide newcomers with valuable background
knowledge. Bilingual school staff or
community members may be able to help.

Good Books

1 _____
2 _____
3 _____
4 _____
5 _____

- **Build a support network.** Children may benefit in several ways from developing their English proficiency skills with the help of someone who speaks their home language. Bilingual tutors or classroom aides can clarify assignments or lesson content for language learners without disrupting the day's activities. Similarly, family members who volunteer to help in the classroom can greatly lessen students' anxiety levels. In addition, each family can support and reinforce class instruction with the student at home.

- **Help children transfer their writing skills.** For English learners who have developed any emergent writing skills in their home languages, build on these skills by occasionally having them write in both languages. Short sentences and picture labels written in a home language and English help children with writing and English acquisition. Bilingual staff members, parents, and other students may serve as valued language resources.

- **Include culturally relevant assignments.** Try to find readings for students that refer to their home cultures. Literature about the home cultures can help keep students' interest level and engagement high. If possible, have students respond to these readings in writing, whether in a journal or a dictated report. If writing skills are limited, encourage students to show their understanding by reporting orally and creating illustrations.

While it may take some time for English language learners to gain proficiency in academic English, newcomers need not feel like outsiders for very long.

Notes

Sheltering Instruction for English Language Learners

What is sheltered instruction?

Sheltered instruction is a combination of strategies for teaching academic content to English language learners at the same time that they are developing proficiency in the English language. This approach to instruction is called *sheltered* because it offers a haven, or refuge, for students who must comprehend subject matter presented in a language they are still learning. Sheltered instruction supports English learners who do not have grade-level academic vocabulary or the familiarity with the American school system that their English-speaking classmates have. It provides extended English language support that English learners receive as they learn subject-area concepts.

How does sheltered instruction help students and teachers?

Sheltered instruction offers practical, easy-to-implement strategies that teachers can use in a mainstream classroom. Many strategies will already be familiar to teachers; what is different is the emphasis sheltered instruction places on extending and scaffolding instruction about the English language. This approach allows teachers to adapt common teaching methods to teach the required content. At the same time, sheltered instruction helps English language learners find the keys they need to make sense of teaching in English about the concepts and processes they need to perform grade-level work in all subjects.

Teachers can help students build mental bridges to new concepts and learning in English by encouraging them to connect their prior knowledge—the diverse skills, experiences, language, and cultural knowledge that they bring to the classroom—to their new learning activities. Finding ways for students to draw on their home language, cultural background, and prior experience can facilitate each English learner's ability to grasp and retain abstract ideas and grade level vocabulary. Finding connections between what they are learning and what they already know in their home language can motivate students to read, write, listen, and speak in English. As comprehension and vocabulary increase, students can transfer more and more concepts from their home languages into English.

This knowledge transfer can work for teachers, too. As teachers tap students' prior knowledge, the teachers will discover when they need to supply background about American events, customs, and idioms that may be new to English language learners.

Some Basics

1. Use Appropriate Speech (Comprehensible Input)

   ✓ **Enunciate.** Speak slowly and clearly, especially when introducing new content and vocabulary.

   ✓ **Provide wait time.** English learners often need extra time to process questions in English and to formulate responses. Allowing students time to think in English demands both concentration and patience.

   ✓ **Replace complex terms with synonyms that are within students' range of proficiency in English.** Use patterned text, repetition, and questions to help students build and expand concepts in English.

Complex term	Synonyms and sentences
Transportation	Car, bus, train, airplane
	Transportation moves people from one place to another place. A car is a type of transportation. A bus is a type of transportation. A train is a type of transportation. What is an airplane? (An airplane is a type of transportation.)

2. Develop Academic Concepts

✓ **Link concepts explicitly to students' prior knowledge and background.** For example, if you introduce a unit on weather, ask students to describe, illustrate, and share what they know about weather. Create and display a class chart that tells about weather in places where students have lived.

Seasons	Kinds of Weather
Puerto Rico	
Rainy season	Rain
Dry season	Sunshine
Oregon	
Spring	Rain
Summer	Sunshine
Fall	Wind
Winter	Snow

✓ **Provide links from past learning to new concepts.** Design a hands-on activity to build background knowledge for new information. For example, introduce the idea of touch (The Five Senses) by having students touch objects with different textures as you introduce the words *soft* (sponge) and *hard* (pencil).

Soft	Hard
sponge	pencil

Give pairs of students a bag of small objects, and have them sort the objects by texture, naming the textures as they sort the objects. Make a wall chart on which you list the objects and the categories into which students sorted them. Include a visual image or drawing next to each word for extra support. Leave the chart on display for students.

✓ **Use supplementary materials.** Storybooks and picture books can clarify and support concept learning. Use picture books that show terms that are hard to explain, such as *covered wagons, rations,* or the *Pony Express.*

3. Emphasize and Develop Key Vocabulary

✓ **Repeat key words, phrases, and concepts, and have students practice using them.** Use "think-pair-share," a discussion strategy developed by Frank Lyman of the University of Maryland and his colleagues, to help students use vocabulary. Have students think of a response to a question using the target vocabulary, share the response with a partner, and report the partner's ideas to the whole group.

✓ **Provide feedback on students' language use.** Use gestures to indicate understanding, as well as supportive questions to prompt students to provide more details.

✓ **Introduce and practice target words in meaningful contexts.** For example, use a hands-on activity to unlock the meaning of the words and to lay the foundation for understanding their application in a specific content area.

4. Connect Written and Oral Language

✓ **Have students repeat words. Give students extra time and opportunities to practice new words and skills.** Vocabulary games and simple crossword puzzles posted on chart paper can help reinforce students' experiences with written and oral language.

✓ **Have students say and write target words to practice and connect written and oral language.** Have students create personal dictionaries to record these words as they say them and include simple drawings to represent the meanings of the words.

Word	Drawing	Meaning (Home Language)
tent		*tienda de campaña*

✓ **Use audiotapes to develop fluency, accuracy, and language acquisition.** Have students listen to audiotapes of books, poetry, or dialogues as a whole group, in pairs, or individually at work stations.

5. Use Visuals, Dramatization, and Realia (Real Things)

✓ **Use word and picture cards to explain vocabulary and content.** Have students make vocabulary note cards that they can use individually or with partners to quiz themselves.

✓ **Use picture walks to preview text, concepts, and vocabulary—and to build background knowledge.** Point out titles, captions, charts, and any visuals in the text that may give clues about the main idea(s) of the reading selections.

✓ **Use demonstrations to show students the instructions and steps they will follow during an activity.** Use realia to provide context for the vocabulary and concepts (for example, pint measure, cup measure, tablespoon, teaspoon). Use graphic organizers, diagrams, drawings, charts, and maps to help students conceptualize information that is abstract or difficult to understand.

✓ **Use Total Physical Response (TPR) for active learning, so that students can show comprehension through physical movement.** For example, have students hear and follow instructions: "Clap your hands for Carla." "Go to the board, and circle the noun with a red piece of chalk."

6. Use a Variety of Questioning Strategies

✓ **Use "think alouds" to model the kinds of question-asking strategies that students use to construct meaning from the text as they read.** Write the 5 W's (Who? What? When? Where? Why?) on a wall chart, and remind students to use these questions as they read to help them understand the text.

✓ **Have students use double entry journals.** Students write their questions on the left-hand pages and their responses to the questions on the right-hand pages.

7. Ongoing Formal and Informal Assessment

✓ **Assess early to understand a student's language level and academic preparedness.** For example, use a K-W-L chart, and allow English learners to illustrate their responses if they cannot use the vocabulary or language structure yet. Encourage students to add words and, if possible, sentences to their illustrations.

✓ **Provide various ways to demonstrate knowledge, including acting, singing, retelling, demonstrating, and illustrating.**

✓ **Use a variety of formal assessments such as practice tests, real tests, and both oral and written assessments.** Use multiple choice, cloze, and open response formats to help students become familiar with various assessment formats.

Sheltered instruction provides English learners with many opportunities to understand and access content area learning. Within this kind of instruction, teachers support English language learning by providing activities that integrate reading, writing, listening, and speaking. Teachers can address the range of cultural, linguistic, and literacy experiences that English learners bring to the classroom by using students' experiences and prior knowledge as topics for these activities. In this way, sheltered instruction can provide students with keys to unlock the doors to comprehension, providing access to both content and language learning.

What Reading Teachers Should Know About Language

Why do reading teachers need to know about the structure of language?

English language learners are entering U.S. classrooms in steadily increasing numbers. The demands on teachers also are surging. To communicate effectively with these students, teachers need to know how to make their instructional talk more comprehensible. Reading teachers need to better understand their students' attempts at written and spoken language.

> "As reading teachers, we have to help children who are beginning to speak English but who are not succeeding with it in academic settings. By learning more about how English works, we discover and improve our strategies for helping children speak, listen to, read, and write English."
>
> — *Terri Murray, elementary teacher*

To improve children's literacy skills in English, teachers must understand how language works *in education*. What should we know about English and other languages? What truths about language help teachers as communicators, as guides, as evaluators, and as advocates for children?

Knowledge about the structure of languages—and particularly of English—is vital not only to linguists and ESL teachers. Reading teachers, too, can make practical, everyday use of the concepts that are posed and explored by the following questions. The answers here can provide beginnings for educators who will help English language learners achieve comprehension as readers, writers, listeners, and speakers of English.

What are the basic units of language?

Spoken language consists of units of different sizes:

Phonemes

Phonemes are the individual sounds in a word that affect meaning. The word *cat* consists of these three phonemes: /k/ /a/ /t/.

Different languages use different sets of phonemes. English language learners may not be familiar with some English phonemes and may need help recognizing and producing these sounds.

Phonemes signal different word meanings. For example, the different vowel sounds in the words *hit* and *heat* indicate that these are two different words.

TiP English language learners who cannot distinguish between the sounds /i/ and /ē/ may not initially recognize that the spoken words *hit* and *heat* are distinct words with different meanings.

Morphemes

Morphemes are the smallest units of meaning in a language. Some morphemes are **free** (or independent) units. Words such as *dog, jump,* and *happy* are free morphemes. Other morphemes are **bound** (or attached), such as inflected endings, prefixes, and suffixes:

- the noun ending -*s* in *dogs*
- the verb ending -*ed* in *jumped*
- the prefix *un-* in *unhappy*
- the adjective ending -*er* in *happier*
- the suffix -*ness* in *happiness*

These bound morphemes add meaning and, in fact, form new words.

TiP English has many kinds of bound morphemes. English learners need to learn how different bound morphemes change the meanings of words.

Words

A word consists of one or more morphemes. A word also can be defined as a meaningful group of morphemes. Native English speakers may pronounce words in ways that make it difficult for English learners to hear word boundaries. For example, in conversation, an English speaker may ask, "Did you eat?"—but pronounce it like "Jeet?"

Some languages use bound morphemes (for example, word endings) to convey the meanings of certain functional English words such as the prepositions *in, on,* and *between.* English learners may need explicit instruction in order to use these functional words correctly. On the other hand, an English word such as *in* may seem familiar to a Spanish speaker who uses the similar preposition *en.*

Phrases

A phrase is a group of words that have meaning together but do not include a subject and a predicate. Since some languages allow the subject or verb to be understood, children may believe that certain phrases in English are equivalent to sentences.

Sentences

A sentence is a meaningful group of words that includes a subject and a predicate. English language learners may understand the concept of sentences, but they may apply word order conventions from their home languages. They also may struggle with the dense sentence structures of academic English.

Discourses

Discourses include speeches, essays, and many other kinds of communication made up of sentences. One kind of discourse frequently heard in U.S. classrooms involves the teacher asking questions and students responding aloud.

TiP Depending on their home cultures, some English learners may find the question-and-response form of discourse unfamiliar.

Why do English learners need to learn about basic units of language?

It helps teachers to understand that units such as bound and free morphemes, words, phrases, and sentences or clauses operate differently in different languages. For example:

- In Chinese, the past tense is not expressed with verb endings, but by separate words that indicate the time of the action (similar to *yesterday* and *already*).

- In Spanish, verb endings indicate the person and number of sentence subjects, so the subject may not be stated in some sentences.

- In Arabic, related words share three-consonant roots. Speakers form related verbs, nouns, and adjectives by applying fixed patterns to these roots and sometimes adding prefixes and suffixes.

English language learners are working mentally to determine how units of English work—as they also try to understand texts and acquire content knowledge.

Depending on their home languages, English learners may already be familiar with some aspects of English, such as certain phonemes and patterns of word order. Other aspects of English will be unfamiliar and will require explicit instruction. For lessons that support challenging concepts in English grammar and phonics, see the Grammar Transition Lessons on pages 62–129 and the Phonics Transition Lessons on pages 130–203.

What is academic English?

Academic English might be described as the language of teachers, literature, textbooks, and content areas, such as science and social studies. Unlike conversational English, academic English is language of a cognitively demanding register, or range. Academic English does not depend as much upon the gestures and circumstances of speech as conversational English does.

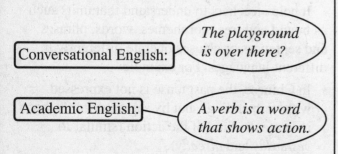

Conversational English: *The playground is over there?*

Academic English: *A verb is a word that shows action.*

Academic English includes content-area vocabulary embedded in complex grammatical structures. It features words about abstract ideas. Understanding this language requires knowledge of content, as well as experience with written materials and classroom discussions.

TIP Many English learners can carry on conversations in English with their native-English-speaking classmates. But they still struggle with reading and writing English—and even understanding their teachers in class. They have acquired social English skills used in personal communication, but they have not yet mastered the academic English used at their grade level.

How do English language learners learn vocabulary?

English language learners must learn much more than the selected vocabulary words in a lesson. They also must make sense of the other unfamiliar words in the lesson—and thousands of other words they continually encounter in school.

Knowing a word involves much more than hearing it and learning its definition. Students must learn how each word relates to its other forms. They gradually learn how it relates to other words and concepts. Knowledge of a word grows during many encounters.

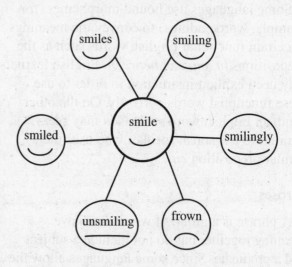

Children learn words in meaningful groups more effectively than in unrelated lists. Look for opportunities to group words in meaningful ways. For example, as children learn the word *invite*, they also can learn *invited, uninvited, invitation, inviting,* and other words in this family. As they learn the word *hippo*, they can learn other animal names, such as *rhino, buffalo,* and *elephant*.

The article "Vocabulary Strategies for Active Learners" begins on page 26.

What is "regular" to English language learners?

Proficient English speakers often take for granted irregularities in English that can puzzle younger and less fluent learners.

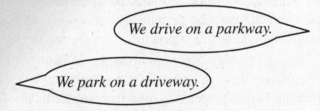

We drive on a parkway.

We park on a driveway.

For example, a child who learns the plural forms *dogs, cats,* and *turtles* may wonder why *mouses, mooses,* and *childs* meet with disapproval. A student who masters these past tense forms—*jumped, walked,* and *stopped*—may try to use *throwed, catched,* or *taked.* In both cases, the child demonstrates an awareness of English conventions, and a teacher should acknowledge this in a positive way. The teacher also should gradually help each student master the many exceptions to the rules.

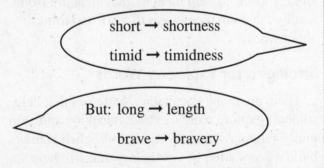

short → shortness

timid → timidness

But: long → length

brave → bravery

Teachers who are aware of the principles of word formation in English can help children acquire vocabulary. English has many helpful patterns for children to learn. Savvy teachers break up the instruction into manageable chunks so that students are not overwhelmed by the many English word patterns they encounter.

What characteristics of written words challenge young English learners?

- Written English is an alphabetic language, and letters represent sounds in words. Languages such as Chinese and Japanese are not alphabetic; written symbols can represent larger parts of words than individual sounds. For students whose home languages are not alphabetic, learning the alphabetic system is an early and continuing challenge.

- The home languages of many English learners—including Spanish, Vietnamese, Hmong, Haitian Creole, and others—are alphabetic. Yet the letter-sound correspondences in these languages are different from those of English. Students can use literacy skills they may have in their home languages, but much new learning is needed to master English.

- While letter-sound correspondences in numerous languages are relatively simple, the relationships of letters to sounds in English can be complicated. In Spanish, for example, the vowel *a* has one sound. In English, *a* can represent many different sounds, as the words *cat, late, saw, Pa, marry, park,* and *dental* begin to illustrate.

- Even in related English words, the same letters can stand for different sounds. Consider *c* in the words *electric, electricity,* and *electrician.* The spelling of these words may challenge children who are learning English, but the shared *c* also indicates the meaningful link among the words.

- The challenges of written English affect not only spelling but also word recognition, comprehension of text, and confidence in language learning.

Many teaching strategies are explored in the Phonics Transition Lessons that begin on page 130 and the article "Effective Writing Instruction for English Language Learners" that begins on page 34.

Vocabulary Strategies for Active Learners

Introduction: Vocabulary Development and English Learners

The National Reading Panel (2000) has identified vocabulary development as a critical component of reading comprehension. Students who lack a well-developed vocabulary—and this includes English language learners—need extra support to extract meaning from the texts they read every day. Research shows that overall, even if they can decode words, English learners struggle with comprehension.

Learning academic vocabulary in English poses challenges for English language learners for many reasons. They are still learning the meaning of words in conversation, basic language structures, and the sounds and spelling of words.

At the same time that students are learning English, they need to keep up with grade-level content area learning, which often uses specialized vocabulary to represent abstract ideas. They may not be able to bring the necessary cultural and background knowledge to the task of unlocking the meaning of English words. For a time, this can obscure context clues that help readers figure out the meanings of new words and ideas. English learners come to school with a wide range of home language literacy, English language proficiency, and previous educational experiences. All of these factors impact their learning in English.

Teachers Support Vocabulary Learning

Teachers can use various strategies to support vocabulary development. These strategies should include helping students encounter and use the vocabulary through meaningful activities in order to understand the concepts behind the words. Students do not learn English words by hearing or seeing them and their definitions once. They need multiple exposures to words. Understanding deepens over time through gradually increased and varied experiences with the words.

For example, think of the word *peach*. A child who has never seen a peach can learn to pronounce the word or decode it in print. Yet the learner will understand the meaning more fully by reading about ripe and juicy peaches, peach pies, peach trees, and perhaps by seeing, touching, and tasting a peach.

English learners need opportunities to learn vocabulary through activities that integrate reading, writing, speaking, and listening skills in the context of meaningful literacy experiences. Language learning is an exploration, and students become "detectives" in search of meaning. Children have a curiosity about learning, and effective teachers nurture this quality through engaging and meaningful activities.

Successful vocabulary learning engages students in active learning, in ways related to meaning. English learners bring diverse experiences, knowledge, and skills to the classroom. Teachers can use what students already know to help them extract meaning from text by teaching them ways to learn and think about words.

Strategies for Exploring Words

There are many vocabulary strategies that help students explore words, extract meaning, and gain understanding. Teachers can help English learners build a foundation of vocabulary that will help them access both language and content area learning.

Related Words

Provide opportunities for English learners to learn new words by grouping words that are related to a specific theme, quality, or activity. Help students classify English words in meaningful categories.

Use word walls, graphic organizers, and concept maps to group related words, record them in meaningful ways, and create visual references that can be used in future lessons.

Teachers can help students group and relate words in different ways, depending on what students can notice and understand, as well as how students will use the vocabulary.

For example, the visual representation below can help students conceptualize that prefixes and suffixes are added on to root words.

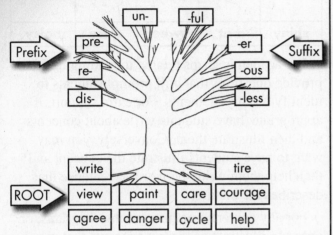

Students can use the diagram above to form words by adding a prefix, a suffix, or both.

Greek and Latin Roots

Technical terms and words for biological structures contain many Greek and Latin roots or combining forms (that is, word parts). Learning the meanings of these roots and word parts can help students figure out content area vocabulary that may be new or abstract. Some students may recognize these roots as parts of words in their home language. They can use this knowledge to figure out the meaning of the root in English, because it is probably the same.

Create and distribute sets of word cards containing Greek and Latin roots. Check if any students know the meaning of a root word before you reveal its meaning. Give an example of an English word containing a Greek or Latin root. Have students find the definition of the word in their dictionaries. Discuss the meaning, and help students connect the meaning of the English word to the meaning of the root word. Extend the

activity by having English learners and native speakers work together in pairs or small groups to build and write other English words containing Greek and Latin roots; you may want each group to focus on a different root. Groups can look up and write the definitions of their words, then share what they learned with the whole group. Create a display of words containing Greek and Latin roots and add to it during the year.

ROOT	MEANING	WORD
aqua (Latin)	water	**aquarium**
art (Latin)	craft, skill	**artist**
aud (Latin)	hear	**audience**
auto (Greek)	self	**autobiography**
bio (Greek)	life	**biography**
duo (Latin)	two	**duet**
geo (Greek)	earth	**geography**
inter (Latin)	among	**intermediate**
octo (Greek)	eight	**octopus**
photo (Greek)	light	**photograph**
pro (Latin)	before, forward	**proceed**
sol (Latin)	sun	**solar**
terra (Latin)	earth	**territory**
unus (Latin)	one	**union**

Cognates

Encourage students to find words that may look or sound similar to words they know in their home languages. Many of these words are cognates—words that have the same or similar meaning in both languages. Recognizing cognates builds on students' background experiences and connects prior knowledge to content area vocabulary and concepts. Be sure students realize that there are false cognates as well—you might call them "false friends"—so they need to check that they have uncovered a true meaning of the word. For example, the English word *actual* and the Spanish word *actual* ("present-day") have quite different meanings.

Point out both true cognates and false cognates as students encounter them in daily work, and record them on a wall chart. Have students create their own cognate/false cognate charts for future reference. (See pages 30–31.)

Multiple-meaning Words

Many English words have multiple meanings. Illustrating and creating examples of the ways words are used can build English learners' experiences and understanding of the multiple meanings that words may have.

Teachers can help students expand their understanding of multiple meanings by sharing sentences, definitions, and pictures that demonstrate the different meanings. For example, contrasting *The pitcher is full of water* with *The pitcher threw the ball,* with illustrations, will help English learners remember the two meanings of *pitcher.*

Illustrate the multiple meanings of words such as *pitcher* or *run* with card sets. (See page 32.) Make sets of word and sentence cards, cut them out, and have students mix the cards and match the meanings. As an extension, have students work with partners, and assign each pair a word for which they will create their own card pair to share with the class. Possibilities include *cold, park, pen, play, roll, sink,* and *stick.*

Academic Language

Developing academic language includes understanding "school language" and a vocabulary of technical terms and abstract meanings. Repeatedly using words and language that are common to various content areas, such as science, social studies, and math, helps English learners connect to the concepts and meanings that the words represent. Teachers can begin by targeting words that are specific to one content area, but are likely to be found in various content learning situations.

Develop vocabulary for describing content area learning by writing adjectives that describe a subject, such as the five senses, and have students add their own words as they use them in activities. Record students' answers on a chart, and have them write their own charts in their journals for reference. To provide extra support, have students illustrate the adjectives they choose.

Sight	Touch	Taste	Smell	Hearing
shiny	hot	sweet	spicy	noisy

For academic terms related to reading itself, provide questions that will prompt students to identify literary elements. For extra support, if appropriate, have students write about concepts and then illustrate them. Conversely, you may want to have students illustrate the concept and then help them write the word or sentence that describes the picture.

For any content area, use graphs, diagrams, or charts to illustrate academic concepts that may be hard to understand abstractly.

Home Language Activities

Teachers can use home language activities to help students reinforce their learning of the concepts and meaning of vocabulary and literacy activities. English learners can participate in a variety of activities, such as discussion, telling or reading stories, listening to songs and music, hearing radio or television weather or sports reports, and interviewing family members, and then use these experiences as topics for discussion and sharing in the classroom. Students can transfer their understanding of a word or concept from their home language to English when they have experiences that illustrate the meaning.

Teachers can find ways to use the home environment as an educational resource by planning activities that involve reading, writing, listening, and speaking about students' family history, culture, and experiences.

Have students use an interview record sheet to illustrate, describe, and write about their conversation with a family member. Help students focus on words in the home language that include *dialogue/conversation/discussion; ask/inquire/interview; tell/answer/respond.* (See page 33.)

Have students use Venn diagrams to record the similarities and differences between their home country or culture and their new home or school setting that includes English. Help students focus on words in the home language that include *similarities/same/alike/compare; differences/ different/contrast; here/there.*

Technology

Teachers can use various forms of technology (computer, Internet, audio, video recording) to meet the specific and varied needs of English learners.

Group Research Report: If appropriate guidance is available, have English learners use the Internet for research on a specific topic related to content learning. For each group, a student recorder can write each team member's Web site and a summary of what they learned.

Have students choose target vocabulary words and illustrate the meanings. With guidance, students can use a search engine or picture-dictionary software to look for images. Then they might print, cut, and paste images into a table. Students can choose their own words while listening to an audio book at home and illustrate them with a table. Use pages to compile a personal dictionary for each student. Have them illustrate academic concepts such as community, transportation, and the seasons.

Word	Class or Dictionary Meaning	Home Language Word	Describe or Draw the Meaning
summer	The season between spring and fall.	Spanish: *el verano* Indonesian: *Musim panas*	

Creating and Adapting Strategies

The great and changing range of ideas, experiences, and needs that English language learners bring to the classroom each day call for teachers to try a variety of strategies to include these students in vocabulary instruction. Savvy teachers recognize that English learners, like all students, respond differently to instructional tactics. The truth is that students grow their own vocabularies, supported by the scaffolding that teachers provide. A great deal of reading in English, listening to selections read aloud, and conversing in English will help learners acquire thousands of words per year if they are engaged in learning, and if teachers do not give up on them. Continue the instructional strategies that work, adapt (or discontinue) the ones that are not effective, and try new approaches as needed.

References

Bear, Donald R., *et al.* (1996). *Words Their Way: Word Study for Phonics, Vocabulary, and Spelling Instruction.* Upper Saddle River, NJ: Prentice Hall.

Blachowicz, Camille L. Z., and Peter Fisher (2002). *Teaching Vocabulary in All Classrooms.* Upper Saddle River, NJ: Prentice Hall.

Center for the Improvement of Early Reading Achievement (2001). *Put Reading First: The Research Building Blocks for Teaching Children to Read.* Washington, DC: Partnership for Reading.

National Reading Panel (2000). *Teaching Children to Read: An Evidence-Based Assessment of the Scientific Research Literature on Reading and Its Implications for Reading Instruction.* Washington, DC: National Institute of Child Health and Human Development.

Vocabulary Development for Reading Success (2004), Scott Foresman Professional Development Series, Module 6. Glenview, IL: Scott Foresman.

Name _____

Cognates

These related words sound similar in two or more languages.
The meanings are the same.

English	Home Language
music	*música* (Spanish) *musika* (Russian)
school	*szkoła* (Polish) *escuela* (Spanish)

© Pearson Education, Inc.

Name _____

False Cognates

These related words sound similar in two or more languages.
The meanings are not the same.

English	Home Language
soap	*sopa* (Spanish)

Name _____

Multiple-meaning Words

 pitcher	**The <u>pitcher</u> is full of water.**
 pitcher	**The <u>pitcher</u> threw the ball.**
ruler	**She is the <u>ruler</u> of the country.**
ruler	**I use a <u>ruler</u> to measure things.**

ELL and Transition Handbook

Interview Record Sheet

Interviewer _____   Date _____

Person interviewed _____

Question:	
Answer:	
Question:	
Answer:	
Question:	
Answer:	
Question:	
Answer:	
Question:	
Answer:	
Question:	
Answer:	
Question:	
Answer:	
Question:	
Answer:	

Effective Writing Instruction for English Language Learners

The Role of Writing in Language and Literacy Development

To provide effective writing instruction for English learners, teachers need to understand how language, literacy, and culture are related (Fillmore and Snow, 2000). When teachers understand how students' home languages and cultural backgrounds can influence how they write and how they understand writing, teachers can find effective ways to meet the instructional needs of these children.

Research shows that children acquire language most readily when they are fully involved in all learning activities in the classroom. Classroom activities should integrate reading, writing, listening, and speaking, as these language skills develop interdependently. This approach supports English language development in the context of meaningful instructional content. That is, students will learn to write (in English) about real ideas and things.

Teachers can facilitate students' language learning and literacy development by ensuring that:

- students hear language in natural ways, in real and practical contexts—and write it in structured formats
- activities in which students participate regularly provide opportunities for listening and speaking so students can internalize the language
- opportunities for acquiring new vocabulary are always present in reading activities and environmental print and are related to the content areas of the curriculum
- opportunities are always available for interesting conversations with English-speaking peers
- mistakes are accepted as part of learning
- students understand why they are being asked to complete various oral communication, reading, and writing tasks

English learners who are already literate, or are emergent readers and writers in their home languages, no doubt have been influenced by their backgrounds and experiences with writing genres, writing styles, and cultural discourse. By learning more about the characteristics of English learners' literacy experiences, teachers can recognize when children are transferring what they already know to their new literacy learning in English, and teachers can support these efforts. It is helpful to seek information about the children in sensitive ways, appropriately respecting families' privacy and regarding home languages and cultures with respect.

Such efforts to find out students' strengths and needs are worthwhile. For example, teachers who compare spelling patterns between a home language and English will better understand the efforts students make to acquire and write English words. Teachers can point out the differences and similarities so that students can learn to compare the languages and develop metalinguistic understanding about how both languages work. This will help them sort out the ways they can use language in their writing.

ENGLISH	celebration	*-tion*
SPANISH	celebración	*-ción*

Some English learners also are emergent writers. For beginning writers, it can help to include both words and pictures in early writing. Experts in English language learning advise teachers to have students write words and attempt sentences to accompany their pictures. Including language provides vital opportunities for students to practice with English.

Scaffolding the Steps of the Writing Process

Writing, whether in a home language or especially in a new language, is the most difficult mode of language use to master (Collier and Ovando, 1998). Each English learner has a unique background and set of experiences with language, literacy, and culture. Students access writing instruction at varying levels of English proficiency. It is important for teachers to provide each child with challenging work that is appropriate for his or her level of English proficiency and literacy. This kind of scaffolding (Vygotsky, 1978) can provide students access to effective instruction.

By understanding the specific kinds of support English learners need at each stage of the writing process, teachers can tailor their instruction to fit individual needs. The following below provides suggestions to help teachers do this.

Structured Writing

Teachers can use **structured writing** to scaffold writing instruction. Structured writing aids include sentence frames and graphic organizers, which help students record and organize their ideas. Teachers need to adjust their expectations for writing to fit students' levels of English proficiency.

	Beginner	Intermediate	Advanced
Prewrite	Allow extra time for prewriting. Use brainstorming, story mapping, dramatization, peer conferencing, or drawing and illustrating.	Allow extra time for prewriting. Use brainstorming, story mapping, peer conferencing, word mapping, or story telling.	Allow extra time for prewriting. Use brainstorming, story mapping, peer conferencing, word mapping, interviews, and reading.
Draft	Student writes words and phrases. Help student turn these into sentences. Accept phonetic invented spelling, but show correct spelling, capitalization, and punctuation.	Student writes words, phrases, and simple sentences. Help student turn phrases into sentences. Accept phonetic invented spelling, but show correct spelling, capitalization, and punctuation.	Student writes phrases, sentences, and paragraphs, with some spelling, capitalization, and punctuation errors; show correct spelling, capitalization, and punctuation.
Revise	Student revises work with the aid of a checklist that has visual clues about each task.	Student revises work with the aid of a checklist that has a written description of each task. Help student incorporate written or oral commentary in revisions.	Student revises work with the aid of a checklist that has a written description of each task—and asks for clarification. Help student incorporate comments in revisions.
Edit	Student uses dictionary to find the correct spelling of a word. Help student use error correction by peer or teacher to make changes.	Student uses dictionary to find the correct spelling of a word. Uses resources such as word bank, word wall, or thesaurus to improve writing. Help student use error correction by peer or teacher to make changes.	Student uses dictionary to find the correct spelling of a word. Uses resources such as word bank, word wall, or thesaurus to improve writing. Clarify error correction by peer or teacher to make changes, and help student incorporate suggestions into writing.
Publish	Student creates final product of writing that reflects revisions and editing process.	Student creates final product of writing that reflects revisions and editing process.	Student creates final product of writing that reflects revisions and editing process.

Summaries

The following scaffolded activity can be used for writing a summary in all subject areas. It can be adapted to meet the needs of beginning, intermediate, and advanced English learners.

- Provide copies of the organizer blackline master on page 39.

- Have students record the important ideas from a read aloud or something they have viewed (beginners); a paragraph or short passage they have read, heard, or viewed (intermediate); a selection students have read, heard, or viewed (advanced).

- Review the five questions on the Organizer with students. Tell them that asking themselves these questions during and after hearing, reading, or viewing the selection, and recording their ideas, will help them recall and think about the selection.

- Encourage students to use English words, drawings, and/or their home language to record their responses to the five questions.

- Tell students to use their notes in the "Write It" column to write a summary on a separate paper, which might be called a Summary/Main Idea sheet. Ask them to write words (beginner), phrases or simple sentences (intermediate), or a paragraph (advanced).

- Encourage all students to use their drawings and their home language responses to help them create summaries in English that express what they learned.

- Finally, ask students to use their summaries to decide what is the main idea of the selection. Have them write the word/phrases/sentences on the Summary/Main Idea paper.

Writing Assignments for English Learners

There are various assignments and activities that encourage English learners to use their background knowledge and previous experiences to connect with the writing process. Establishing a daily or weekly **routine** for these assignments and activities helps cue students about what to expect and provides extra support for participating meaningfully in classroom instruction.

Teachers can compile a **writing portfolio** to show progress over time, and to facilitate home communication and teacher/student dialogue about writing.

Language Experience Approach

Students dictate stories to the teacher (or aide), who writes them down. Students then copy the words that the teacher wrote. In this way, reading and writing become processes that are directly related to students' experiences. Students read and write to express themselves and communicate their experiences.

Dialogue Journals

Dialogue journals develop writing skills and provide authentic communication between student and teacher. This writing is informal and may include pictures. It allows the student to choose his or her topics for writing. The teacher may suggest topics, but students' choices encourage active learning. The teacher responds to the content of each student's writing, also in a conversational manner. Writing errors are not explicitly corrected, but the teacher's writing serves as a model (Collier and Ovando, 1998).

Home Literacy Activities

Home literacy activities encourage conversation between students and their family members as they read together in their home language and/or English. For parents who are not literate, students can practice reading aloud and discussing stories with them. Teachers can plan activities such as having students interview family members in the home language and then share the responses with the class in English.

Writing Products

While there are a variety of authentic writing assignments that encourage students to write about their interests and experiences, there are specific genres with which students must become familiar in order to build an understanding of text structures that reflect district and state standards or curriculum frameworks. The following chart suggests ways to approach each genre in relation to English learners' needs. The blackline masters on pages 40–42 can be used to help English learners develop specific writing products.

Personal Narrative	Have students choose a meaningful experience to write about. Have students illustrate the event or bring in a picture of the event. Use a **concept web** to help students brainstorm the details related to the event, and allow room, if necessary, for drawing/illustrating specific ideas and details that students may not yet be able to express in English. Use **writing frames** to help students write paragraphs that represent the ideas they brainstorm with pictures, words/phrases/sentences.
Story	Have students use a **story sequence** map (see page 40) to brainstorm ideas for writing a story. Ask students to use words, but allow them to use illustrations as well. Provide **writing frames** to create sentences that represent the scenes (In the beginning _____, etc.). Have students use a **character web** to develop the characteristics of the main character(s), and help students make a **word bank** of adjectives they can use to describe these characteristics. Do a read aloud and use a **story elements chart** to record story elements from a read aloud (in English and/or students' home languages if possible) to reinforce the concepts of setting, characters, problems, and important events of a story.
How-to Report	Have students choose an activity that they or someone in their family knows how to do well. Ask students to use a **sequence map** (see page 41) to record all the steps of the activity. Encourage students to write the steps in their home language first, if necessary. Provide students with **writing frames** to insert words/phrases/sentences from their notes to create a How-to Report.
Compare and Contrast Essay	Have students work with partners to discuss their interests and experiences (languages they speak, home country or city, music, food, hobbies, goals for the future). Have partners **interview** each other, using a list of questions that the class brainstorms. Ask them to record what they have in common in the center section of a **Venn diagram** (see page 42). Have them label each outer section with one of their names, and to use those sections to record what they do not have in common. Provide **writing frames** to help students insert information from the Venn diagram into a Compare and Contrast Essay format.
Persuasive Essay	Have students choose a topic or cause they feel strongly about; for example, wearing uniforms in schools, recycling, technology in school, and so on. Make a **problem-solution chart** to state the problem, and brainstorm solutions to the problem. Ask students to use words, but allow them to use illustrations as well. Use **writing frames** to model the step-by-step writing of a persuasive essay. Have students use their own problem-solution charts to write their essays at the same time the teacher models.
Research Report	Allow students to **choose a topic** of interest to research and write about. Provide copies of the summary and main idea organizer blackline master for students to use (page 39). Provide **writing frames,** and use the overhead to **model the step-by-step** research process and report writing. Use **think-alouds** to model the thinking that goes on inside a writer's head when writing a research report.

Rubrics to Evaluate Writing

The sample rubric that follows focuses on one of the traits of good writing, conventions of English. It describes what English learners at various levels (beginner, intermediate, and advanced) would be expected to write in the second half of Grade 5. Teachers can develop similar evaluation forms that reflect the needs of the school, the grade, and the students involved. Other examples of traits of good writing may include Focus/Ideas, Order, Writer's Voice, Word Choice, and Sentences.

Teachers can use school, district, state, or national standards for English learners to create rubrics that adjust expectations for English learners based on their individual English proficiency levels. (See page 43.)

References

Collier, V. P., and C. J. Ovando (1998). *Bilingual and ESL Classrooms: Teaching in Multicultural Contexts*. Boston, MA: McGraw Hill.

Echevarria, J., M. Vogt, and D. Short (2004). *Making Content Comprehensible for English Learners: The SIOP Model*. Boston: Allyn & Bacon.

Fillmore, L. W., and C. E. Snow (2000). *What Teachers Need to Know about Language*. Washington, DC: ERIC Clearinghouse on Languages and Linguistics.

Vygotsky, L. S. (1978). *Mind in Society: The Development of Higher Psychological Processes*. Cambridge, MA: Harvard University Press.

Traits of Good Writing: Conventions (English Learners)

	Capitalization	Punctuation	Sentence Structure and Grammar	Spelling
Beginner (little experience in English)	Uses capitalization when writing one's own name and at the beginning of sentences.	Adds a period to the end of a sentence and a question mark to the end of a question.	Begins to use some standard word order, with mostly inconsistent grammatical forms (for example, subject/verb agreement).	Produces some independent writing that includes inconsistent spelling.
Intermediate (conversational but not academic English)	Uses capitalization to begin sentences and proper nouns.	Produces independent writing that may include some inconsistent use of periods and question marks.	Uses standard word order but may use inconsistent grammatical forms.	Produces independent writing that includes some misspelling.
Advanced (gaining skills in academic English)	Produces independent writing with consistent use of correct capitalization.	Produces independent writing with generally consistent use of correct punctuation.	Uses complete sentences and generally correct word order.	Produces independent writing with consistent use of correct spelling.

Name _____

Organizer: Summary and Main Idea

ASK	DRAW	IN OTHER WORDS (English or Home Language)	WRITE
Who?			_____ _____ _____
What?			_____ _____ _____
When?			_____ _____ _____
Where?			_____ _____ _____
Why?			_____ _____ _____

Story Sequence Map

Title _____

	In the beginning	In the middle	At the end

Name _____

How-to Sequence Map

How to _____

Draw It ✏️

First _____

_____

⬇

Draw It ✏️

Next _____

_____

⬇

Draw It ✏️

Last _____

_____

Name _____

Compare and Contrast Venn Diagram

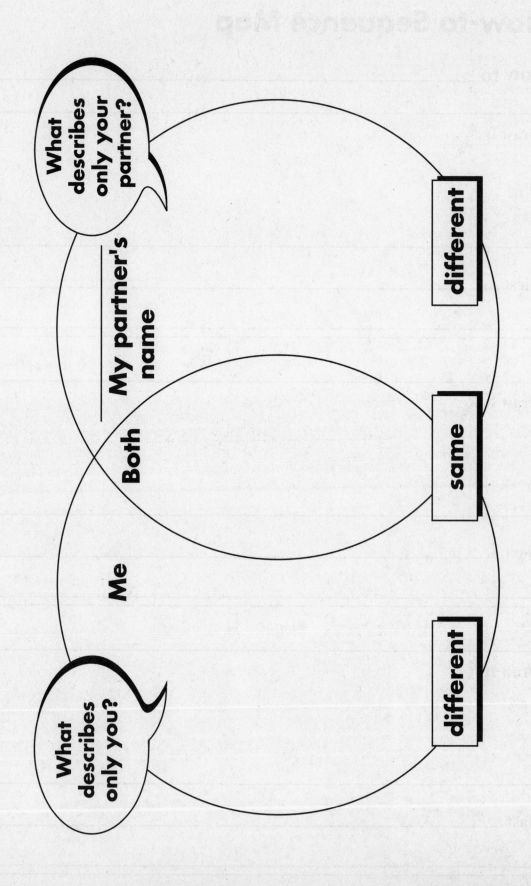

What describes
only your partner?

My partner's
name

different

Both

same

Me

different

What
describes
only you?

A Trait of Good Writing: _____
(English Learners)

_____ (trait)	_____	_____	_____
Beginner (little experience in English)	(Uses/Produces/Creates _____) _____ _____ _____ _____	(Uses/Produces/Creates _____) _____ _____ _____ _____	(Uses/Produces/Creates _____) _____ _____ _____ _____
Intermediate (conversational but not academic English)	(Uses/Produces/Creates _____) _____ _____ _____ _____	(Uses/Produces/Creates _____) _____ _____ _____ _____	(Uses/Produces/Creates _____) _____ _____ _____ _____
Advanced (gaining skills in academic English)	(Uses/Produces/Creates _____) _____ _____ _____ _____	(Uses/Produces/Creates _____) _____ _____ _____ _____	(Uses/Produces/Creates _____) _____ _____ _____ _____

Promoting Cultural Affirmation and Family Involvement

Research shows that a school curriculum that includes topics about students' cultures and experiences helps engage and motivate English learners. Teachers can use a variety of best practices to promote cultural affirmation and to draw upon parental involvement that supports children's learning.

- **Reflect Students' Cultures and Languages**
Develop active learning and connections with the curriculum through the use of students' home cultures and, if possible, home languages. Plan reading, writing, speaking, and listening activities with texts that reflect students' personal interests, cultures, prior experiences, and background knowledge.

- **Link Curriculum to Home Resources**
Create ways to use the home environment as an educational resource. Make connections between content area learning and the home through activities that depend on the expertise of family members. Use families' home languages and daily activities, such as cooking, cleaning, working, traveling, and playing, as a basis for learning.

- **Encourage Family Literacy** Plan family literacy activities that require students to interact with family members in the home language. Create a variety of activities such as discussion, telling or reading stories, listening to music or radio, and interviewing family members. Use these experiences as topics for discussion and sharing in the classroom.

- **Create School-Home Partnerships**
Encourage parents to participate in their children's learning by planning school events that reflect the needs of parents or guardians of English learners. Plan activities and opportunities that show parents how they can use their home languages, their experiences, and their expertise both in the classroom and at home.

Family and Home as Educational Resources

- Get to know students' home lives and cultures by using everyday life and culture as topics for activities in class. Encourage storytelling and oral tradition by having students use their home languages to interview parents, grandparents, and immediate family members and then inviting students to share the stories with the class. Keep a portfolio of all the reading, writing, speaking, and listening activities that use students' home experiences, and compile them in binders that students can take home and show to their families.

- Use home activities for teaching concepts such as "following steps in a process" (for example, how to make something) and "giving directions." Ask students to find a special talent of a family member (for example, building or fixing something; singing, dancing, or playing a musical instrument; quilting, embroidering, or artwork; or cooking). Ask students to record (by writing notes or making pictures) the steps the family member performs. Help them turn their notes into instructions that other people can follow. Compile all the instructions in a class book to share with classmates and families.

- Create a class mural or quilt that represents the home cultures and languages of students. Send home a panel for a mural or quilt, and ask the family to represent their culture and language through the use of visuals and/or writing. Encourage families to illustrate their special experiences and personalities (for example, by using a map of their home country, a family picture, words in the home language, artwork, or a souvenir or pictures from their home country and their travels). Hang the quilt or mural where parents can see it when they visit the school.

- Assign activities that include the use of families' home languages. These activities and assignments can utilize the home languages as well as the language of instruction, English. Have students ask family members for examples of popular sayings in their home languages that teach a lesson or moral, and share the meaning of these sayings with the class. Help students express the meaning of each home-language saying in English through words and a drawing that illustrates the main point. Use a two-column chart to record students' sayings, and then brainstorm sayings that express similar meanings in English. Make a multilingual book of class sayings to share with classmates and families.

Bridging the Curriculum and Home

- Plan family curricular events that combine social and curriculum-related themes when parents can come to see their children's presentations or projects. Plan hands-on math, science, and social studies related activities in which parents, siblings, and other family members can participate (such as astronomy night, math games, recipe exchange, and health fair). With the help of student journalists and photographers, create a monthly parent newsletter, which includes pictures and descriptions of the kinds of activities children do in the different content areas.

- During parent conferences, home visits, or family events, provide information about daily class routines, and describe the classroom and school expectations for learners. List the strategies that will help children succeed in the classroom setting. Give examples of what the classroom expectations are, model how students should achieve them, and give students time to practice the strategies during appropriate times. Give parents and families information about ways they can support their children's learning at home (for example, *Ask your child to describe the activities he or she did in school; provide a quiet place where your child can do homework*). Send this kind of information to families in the home languages, and take time to discuss and review it at parent conferences and activities. Resources for home languages may include bilingual school staff, community members, and the families themselves.

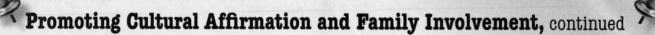

- Send a brief survey home to parents to find out more about their specific needs and concerns, and use this information to plan topics for family-based school events. Based on families' responses, invite guest speakers who speak the home languages of the families, to give informational presentations about the topics of interest to families. Such activities tell families that the school is responsive to the needs of both students and their families as a whole, and that education is a partnership between home and school.

- Invite willing and able parents to be classroom helpers so they can learn how their children are taught specific subjects. Parent helpers then can reinforce at home the kinds of learning their children experience during school days. Parents can help the teacher and students during activities, can use their home languages to explain and assist, and can share relevant expertise with the class.

Links to Home Languages and Cultures

- Help children create dual-language books. Newcomers or beginners can write in their home languages; encourage students to gradually move into English, as they are able to do so. Such books can provide outreach to families with ranges of literacy backgrounds and can encourage students to make connections between their home languages and English.

- For math-related activities, collect and graph information about families' home countries or languages. Students can carry out interviews in the home language with family members and use target vocabulary and language for reporting information. Use a variety of graphs (bar, pie, and other kinds) to record information, and send class graphs home to share with families.

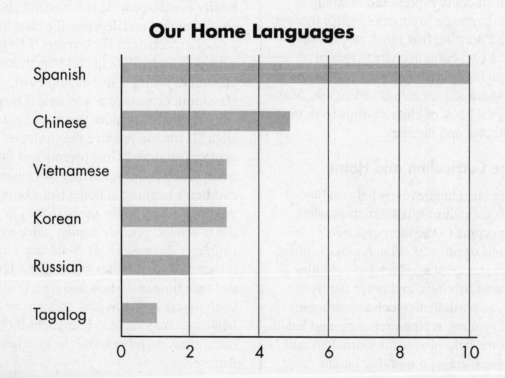

Our Home Languages

- Include family history, culture, and experiences as topics for projects. Have students interview family members and create a biography project. Invite children to include pictures, drawings, and stories that tell about families' home countries or cultures, ancestors, and customs. Celebrate by inviting families to school to share and read each others' biographies.

- Make "book bags" with audiobooks in home languages, and send them home to encourage family story activities. Encourage all family members to participate in home literacy activities. Provide a simple list of questions that families can discuss at home, and then ask students about their discussions.

References

August, D., and K. Hakuta. 1997. *Improving Schooling for Language Minority Children: A Research Agenda*. Washington, DC: National Academy Press.

Collier, V., and W. Thomas. 1992. A Synthesis of Studies Examining Long-Term Language Minority Student Data on Academic Achievement. *Bilingual Research Journal* 16(1-2): 187-212.

Cummins, J. 2000. *Language, Power, and Pedagogy*. Clevedon: Multilingual Matters.

Fillmore, L. W., and C. E. Snow. 2000. *What Teachers Need to Know about Language*. Washington, DC: ERIC Clearinghouse on Languages and Linguistics.

Freeman, Y. S., and D. E. Freeman. 2002. *Closing the Achievement Gap*. Portsmouth, NH: Heinemann.

Suárez-Orozco, C., and M. M. Suárez-Orozco. 2001. *Children of Immigration*. Cambridge, MA: Harvard University Press.

Helping the Helpers

Teacher assistants or aides, classroom volunteers, tutors, and classmates can provide important, ongoing support to students acquiring English. This support can be invaluable in helping students improve their proficiency.

How Can Teachers Recruit Helpers?

Invite parents, family members, school staff, and community members to be classroom helpers, in accordance with school or district policies. Contact community agencies that may coordinate and place volunteers in schools. Keep parents and the community updated through newsletters and announcements at school events about the specific opportunities and needs you have. College and university schools of education may be a good place to advertise volunteer opportunities, as students earning their teaching licensure are often interested in gaining experience in working with English learners.

You might use a school Web site to announce that you are looking for bilingual volunteers or for native English speakers who can spend time helping English learners improve their ability to read and write in English. You might identify students in your class who can show English learners certain classroom procedures, check that they understand activity instructions correctly, or listen to them read and help them with both pronunciation and comprehension. These peer helpers may include advanced English language learners who have acquired enough proficiency in English to offer help.

How Can Home Languages Be Used to Support English Learners?

Helpers who know the same home language as English learners can support instruction by clarifying key concepts and vocabulary and by reinforcing instructions and procedural information. Simultaneous or direct translation of what the teacher says is not recommended, since students should be listening to the teacher and pushing themselves to understand as much as they can. The helper, however, can listen with the student, check what the student understands, confirm what is correct, and add any details he or she may have missed. Volunteers also can use the home language to provide background knowledge that will help the student understand the overall meaning. Helpers also can use the home language as a way to connect classroom learning with students' prior experiences and cultural background.

Strategies for Classroom Instruction

The following chart lists a few strategies that volunteers can use when working with English learners. In the chart, L1 (Language 1) refers to the English learner's home language. When possible, find volunteers who know the home language of English learners. These volunteers can provide assistance to teachers and schools by communicating important instructional clarification to both the students and their families. Bilingual volunteers can facilitate the understanding of expectations and instructions, and they can provide clarification of subject matter concepts. Home language tutors also can provide information about the child's learning in the home language that will help the teacher more accurately assess the child's learning. Volunteers who primarily know the child's home language can provide support for the classroom teacher by developing children's home language literacy and learning skills, which will eventually transfer into English.

Adult Volunteer or Aide Helping in English	Adult Volunteer or Aide with L1 and English Fluency	Peer Helpers with L1, English, or Both	Adult Volunteer or Aide Helping Primarily in L1
____ Speak clearly and slowly. Learn to pronounce students' names correctly.	____ Support content-area learning by clarifying the meaning of concepts and vocabulary, in English and the home language.	____ Help students understand classroom rules and routines and the English terms and phrases associated with them. Show students how to follow teacher instructions.	____ Support students with reading, writing, speaking, and listening activities in the home language.
____ Use picture cards or other visuals to introduce and practice vocabulary.	____ Support hands-on activities by reinforcing teachers' instructions in English and in students' home language as needed.	____ Explain teacher's instructions or expectations in the home language.	____ Record audio books for home-language book bags that can be used as home-language literacy activities.
____ Model pronunciation of new words and phrases, and have students repeat several times.	____ Support communication with families by calling home to invite parents to school events, to remind them of important events such as picture day, and to provide details such as information about field trips.	____ Model reading, writing, listening, and speaking activities in English when working with partners or in small groups.	____ Model storytelling in the home language, and encourage and listen to students' own storytelling in the home language.
____ Use gestures, pictures, and objects when you give explanations to enhance understanding.		____ Convey questions or concerns that a newcomer may have to the teacher and communicate the teacher's answer to the student.	____ Find ways to share the students' home culture and experiences with the teacher and classmates. Encourage projects such as a collage, a display, or another visual representation of the students' home culture.
____ Give students extra time to understand your instructions or a question, and to give a response.			
____ Read books with simple, repetitive, natural language that students can learn to read and use independently.	____ Facilitate communication between English learners and the teacher when students need help expressing themselves in English.	____ Be patient and encourage partner to keep trying. Smile!	

English Language Learners and Assessment

Assessment Needs of Diverse Learners

Because English language learners make up a dynamic group of learners who enter school with a wide range of linguistic, cultural, and learning experiences, it is important for teachers to learn about the unique background of each individual learner. Overall, assessment can provide important information about children's learning that can be used to plan appropriate and meaningful instruction. However, the kinds of assessment, the purposes for which they are used, and how the results are evaluated can directly impact how meaningful the assessments are (Cummins, 1981).

High-stakes Testing vs. Authentic Assessment

While so-called "high-stakes" testing has become increasingly influential, high-profile tests can be difficult for English learners because they require proficiency in academic English, understanding of grade-level subject matter, and an understanding of cultural contexts. While high-stakes test results in the United States influence instructional decisions made in schools, these results often do not reflect **what** English learners know, and the instructional decisions based on test results often do not reflect the specific learning needs of English learners (Bielenberg and Fillmore, 2005).

It is important to find a variety of ways to assess English language learners that show what each student is able to do. Focusing on what children already know—and what they are learning but have not mastered—helps teachers identify the specific educational needs of students and enables educators to build their ongoing instruction upon all the resources, experiences, and abilities that English learners bring to school. Authentic assessment, or ongoing classroom-based (often informal) assessment of students by

teachers, allows students to show their strengths. Ongoing assessment also provides teachers with an accurate, dynamic picture of how to plan instruction and provide feedback in ways that meet the changing learning needs of each student (García, 1994). Following this approach, teachers can use accurate information about how to plan individualized instruction for English learners that will support their progress, through adaptations and modifications, until they are able to fully access and participate in the target curriculum in English and in assessments such as "high-stakes" tests.

Authentic Assessment Activities

Because English learners exhibit varying levels of English proficiency, it is important during assessment to allow them to express themselves in a variety of ways that do not depend solely on their understanding of English and their abilities to respond in English. The following is one example of this.

Story Retelling

Story retelling that allows students to support their verbal responses by drawing or illustrating details about the story (that is, to **show** the order of events in a story) can help the teacher assess what a student has understood, even if students do not yet have the vocabulary base or English language structures to describe the events in the story.

The following instructions describe how story retelling can be scaffolded, or specially structured, for English learners. It models the concept of sequencing events of a story by demonstrating sequential events with which they are already familiar, such as getting ready for school. This is one way to use informal assessment in order to find out whether individual students understand the concept of sequence, and whether English learners can use the sequence words appropriately to retell a series of events in order.

This story retelling activity also allows English learners to respond and express what they understand, according to their individual language proficiency level, by providing a variety of ways to express their understanding. English learners with beginning proficiency levels may use dramatization, illustrations, words, and possibly phrases to retell, while intermediate and advanced English learners may use a combination of the prior strategies along with sentences and possibly a short paragraph.

The Story Retelling Activity (page 56) that follows the instructions below can be used as a model form to use or adapt in order to meet the needs of students in various grades or with various levels of English proficiency.

Instructions: Story Retelling Activity (page 56)

Tell students that they will use the words *first, next, last* to retell a story that will be read, or viewed in class, and let them know they will tell about the events of the story **in order.** This is one way to provide clear expectations that clue students in to what they will be asked to do, and it also provides background knowledge that can help students understand the story retelling process.

✓ Have each student repeat and practice the words *first, next,* and *last.* Provide an example of the meaning of these words by acting out what you do in the morning to get ready for school: "**First,** I wake up and eat breakfast. **Next,** I brush my teeth. **Last,** I walk out the door to go to school." Ask volunteers to dramatize their own sequence of events (*e.g.,* a school day; shopping at the supermarket; getting ready for bed, etc.). Write the words *first, next, last* on the board or on chart paper, and ask students to say the words as they are acting out their own sequence of events.

✓ After viewing, listening to, and/or reading a story, have students draw or illustrate what happened **first, next,** and **last** in the story they will retell. For each scene illustrated, ask the student to describe what he or she drew. For those students who struggle with expressing their ideas in English, allow them to use their home language or encourage them to act out what they mean, and then write the word, phrase, or sentence that represents what they said in their home language or what they acted out.

✓ If the story has more than three main events, help students use *next* more than once, if necessary.

✓ Record the responses: words (beginners), phrases (intermediate), or sentences (advanced). Finally, have the students copy what they dramatized, expressed in their home language, or dictated for each scene on the lines below each scene. Ask students to repeat and practice the words, phrases, or sentences several times; then have them retell the story to a partner or to the whole group.

✓ For more advanced students, add an extra column for an additional scene after "next" and label it "then" in order to include a more detailed description about the story. Encourage more advanced students to write several sentences for the scene in each column.

✓ As part of ongoing assessment of expressive reading and fluency, use audio equipment to record students' oral readings of the story retelling activity.

✓ To chart students' progress in story retelling, use the Retelling Record teacher form (page 57). To chart students' progress in the retelling of nonfiction selections, first adapt page 56 for students to record ideas, and then use the Retelling Record on page 57.

Reading Fluency and Comprehension Assessment

Authentic assessment focuses on teachers making informed decisions based on authentic literacy tasks within the classroom context that reflect individual students' progress and learning (García, 1994). Finding ways to help English learners develop reading fluency means finding out if students really comprehend what they read, rather than just decode words. Reading comprehension depends on how well a student can extract meaning by making use of various clues in the text. Understanding and using clues in the text requires readers to be familiar with language structures, spelling, grammar, and text structures, and to have background experience and knowledge about the topic of the reading passage.

Students' English language proficiency levels, the kinds of literacy and learning experiences students have had, and how familiar they are with the topic of the reading passage will affect how much they struggle with understanding what they read. Literature also can be challenging for English learners because of the use of figurative language, including metaphors, similes, and symbolism.

When assessing fluency and comprehension, it can help if teachers learn how students' home literacy and languages affect their learning in English. English learners may draw on what they already know; for example, an English learner whose home language is Spanish may use Spanish spelling patterns and/or phonetics when reading words in English. Recognizing the influence of the home language and the student's reliance upon the literacy skills and strategies he or she knows in the home language will help teachers not only assess more accurately, but know how to point out similarities and differences between English and the home

language as a way to develop awareness about how different languages are related. This helps develop metalinguistic awareness, or thinking about how language works.

Teachers must ultimately use all they know about each student's English proficiency and literacy skills in order to:

- monitor progress
- organize students in groups for effective learning
- differentiate instruction

Assessing English learners and learning about their cultural, linguistic, and learning experiences can help teachers become more precise in helping students and in planning instruction that is comprehensible and challenging.

Language Learning Profiles and Anecdotal Records

English language proficiency is acquired along a continuum. Individual learners often are at different places along this continuum, and they progress at different rates, based on a variety of factors, such as proficiency in the home language, prior knowledge of English, similarities between the home language and English, motivation, learning styles, and prior literacy and learning experiences (August and Hakuta, 1997; Cummins, 1981). Because of the varying rates at which students acquire English, it is important for teachers to know and record where on the proficiency continuum each student is at the beginning of the school year (or when the student enters the school) and to keep ongoing observation records of student progress. This will not only help teachers recognize progress, but will also provide information about the specific areas in which English learners need extra support. Following is a general description of the different levels of English language proficiency.

Overview of English Language Proficiency Levels	
Beginning	Beginning English language learners have little vocabulary or literacy in English. This refers only to their English proficiency, which is why it is helpful to learn as much as possible about students' literacy in their home languages.
Intermediate	Intermediate English learners have some conversational fluency in English but still are not proficient in the academic English of books and instruction.
Advanced	Advanced English learners have developed conversational fluency and some literacy/proficiency in academic English at their grade level, but they are not fully proficient and are still building their academic English.

Recording information about a student's proficiency in English and/or the home language can be done with the help of a **Language Proficiency/Literacy/Academic Profile** (see page 58). Checkmarks, notes, and dates can be used to fill in the chart. This form can be adapted to include content-specific or language-specific information. Through conferences with parents, and meetings with teachers, tutors, volunteers, and other specialists that work with English learners, teachers can continue to gather valuable information that will help inform instruction to provide individualized support for each student.

In addition to creating a **Language Proficiency/Literacy/Academic Profile** to gather background information and establish an understanding of the strengths an English learner brings to school, the use of **Anecdotal Records** (see pages 59 and 60) can provide ongoing assessment and information about student learning that can show growth and inform the teacher about specific areas in which a student needs support and reinforcement.

When planning for instruction and assessing English learners, it is important to remember that these students are not only learning grade-level subject area concepts, but they are also learning English language skills—reading, writing, listening, and speaking skills—at the same time. It is important that teachers include what students need to know and what they must be able to do with the language of instruction: vocabulary, language structures, procedural language such as asking questions, expressing hypothesis, describing, identifying, and so on. These language learning goals, or **language objectives,** help English learners develop language as well as content knowledge.

Teachers can use local and state standards developed for English learners and/or new national standards developed, for example, by Teachers of English to Speakers of Other Languages (TESOL), and the World-class Instructional Design and Assessment (WIDA) Consortium, a consortium of states that have created standards that describe what English language learners should be able to do at varying English language proficiency levels to achieve subject area learning. These standards can be used with the Anecdotal Records (page 60) under the "Skills" section to document reading, writing, speaking, and listening skills observed by the teacher.

Scaffolding High-stakes Testing

While "high-stakes" testing presents various challenges for English learners, there are various test-taking strategies that teachers can use to support students in preparing for eventual mastery of standardized testing. Showing students ways in which they can recognize test formats and decode the questions of a test will help them figure out what each question is asking them to do. Outcome based/norm referenced tests are different from ongoing authentic assessment because they evaluate, or make a judgment about, the performance of a student at a given time, while authentic assessment informs both teachers and students about day-to-day learning and provides feedback about how to proceed in order to meet the needs of individual learners.

English learners must be taught test-taking strategies and must build background about the language and procedures of test taking. Use the suggestions on the Test-taking Strategies Teaching Log (page 61) when preparing English learners, who may not be experienced with the specialized language and implications of standardized tests, to unlock the often hidden meaning embedded in test structure and language (Bielenberg and Fillmore, 2005).

Keep a log of ways to improve test-taking experiences for English learners. Refer to your log for future reference, for sharing with colleagues, and for self-assessing instruction for students. (See page 61.)

Here are instructions and examples for preteaching vocabulary and question types.

Preteach Vocabulary and Question Types

- Make a T chart to list the question types students will find on tests. Explain what the structures mean and what they ask students to do.

- Make a short list of test vocabulary, phrases, and instructions students may find on tests, such as *choose, write, fill in the circle, less than, greater than,* and *"that best fits in the sentence."* Illustrate what these phrases ask students to do.

Example:

TEST DIRECTIONS	WHAT SHOULD I DO?
Choose the word that goes in the blank. Mark your answer. 1. My grandfather reads many _____ about his country. ○ storys ○ stories ○ storyis ○ story	**Choose** = pick, decide on one **Blank** = the line 1. My grandfather reads many _____ about his country. • **Mark** = use pencil to fill in the circle

Example:

PHRASE	WHAT DOES IT MEAN?
Express 75% as a decimal.	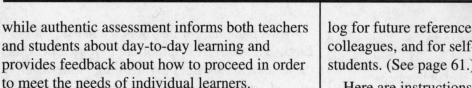 75% percent → as a → .75 decimal

Assessment Accommodations for English Learners

While English learners need time to acquire the academic language necessary to be able to perform well on tests in English, there are some accommodations that may support their attempts at extracting meaning from test language, questions, and passages. Accommodations for English learners may include the following:

- Provide English learners with extra time to complete the test.
- Allow the use of a bilingual dictionary to clarify words that may hinder comprehension.
- Read the question aloud in some cases.
- If possible, give the test in the classroom setting where they receive English learner services (if applicable) to reduce anxiety level.

References

August, D., and K. Hakuta (1997). *Improving Schooling for Language Minority Children: A Research Agenda.* Washington, DC: National Academy Press.

Bielenberg, B., and L. W. Fillmore (2004–2005). The English They Need for the Test. *Educational Leadership, 62*(4), 45–49.

Cummins, J. (1981). The Role of Primary Language Development in Promoting Educational Success for Language Minority Students. In *Schooling and Language Minority Students: A Theoretical Framework.* Sacramento, CA: California Department of Education.

García, G. E. (1994). Assessing the Literacy Development of Second Language Students: A Focus on Authentic Assessment. In K. Spangenbergk-Urbschat and R. Pritchard (Eds.), *Kids Come in All Languages: Reading Instruction for ESL Students* (pp. 180–205). Newark, DE: International Reading Association.

Name _____

Story Retelling

Title _____

First

Next

Last

Retelling Record

Student's Name: _____

Behaviors Observed	Date:			Date:			Date:			Date:		
	Yes	Somewhat	No	Yes	Somewhat	No	Yes	Somewhat	No	Yes	Somewhat	No
Uses selection illustrations or photos to guide the retelling												
Adapts language heard in other retellings for his/her own purposes												
Provides additional information about the selection when questioned												
Fiction												
Identifies main characters and setting												
Describes significant events in the story												
Summarizes the ending of the story												
Nonfiction												
Uses text features such as headings, captions, diagrams, or labels to guide the retelling												
Identifies the main idea of the selection												
Identifies supporting details in the selection												

© Pearson Education, Inc.

Language Proficiency/Literacy/ Academic Profile

Name _____ Grade _____

Home Language(s) _____

ABILITIES	Beginning	Intermediate	Advanced
L1 Listening			
L1 Speaking			
L1 Reading/Writing			
English Listening			
English Speaking			
English Reading/ Writing			
Academic/ Content Skills and Knowledge (English and L1)			

L1= Child's home language other than English

Teacher Form ✓

Anecdotal Record (Sample)

Student Name and Date	Use of Oral English	Use of Written English	Skills	
Date: 5/3/06 **Student Name:** _David_ **English Language Proficiency Level:** ✓ Beginner __ Intermediate __ Advanced	*Asked Ana if he could borrow her marker during writers workshop.*	*Copied friendly letter from overhead; used as a model to write the salutation of his own pen pal letter.*	**READING** *Follows list–instructions for writers workshop activity.*	**WRITING** *Records and labels nouns.*
			LISTENING *Comprehends the high-frequency word "reason".*	**SPEAKING** *Produces words/ phrases to retell story.*

Anecdotal Record

Student Name and Date	Use of Oral English	Use of Written English	Skills	
Date: _____ **Student Name:** _____ **English Language Proficiency Level:** __ Beginner __ Intermediate __ Advanced			**READING**	**WRITING**
			LISTENING	**SPEAKING**

Test-taking Strategies Teaching Log

How have I....?	Dates	Strategies and Activities
Pointed out the text structures and conceptual references used in tests?		
Pointed out difficult language structures, grammar, and spelling?		
Pretaught basic vocabulary and content area vocabulary?		
Built background experience and knowledge about test taking and procedural language?		

Part 2
Grammar Instruction for English Language Learners

Contents

© Pearson Education, Inc.

Introduction to the Grammar Transition Lessons

English language learners have experience mainly with their home languages, and the grammars of different languages vary widely. As these students encounter English, keep in mind that their home languages may differ in aspects such as the following:

- The languages may use different word order than English does.
- They may not use the same parts of speech as English does.
- Their tense structures may be simpler or more complex than English tense structure.
- Nouns and adjectives that are neutral in English may be masculine or feminine in a student's home language.

For teachers, it is vitally helpful to remember that grammar is much more than a set of rules for saying and writing sentences correctly. Grammar primarily consists of the ways that speakers and writers of a language communicate ideas, mainly in sentences. As students learn how English sentences work, along with the meanings of many words, they become able to successfully communicate their ideas. They will gradually learn the rules, read and write the punctuation, and eventually become proficient in the standard English usage that is regarded as correct English.

The core grammar and writing lessons in *Scott Foresman Reading Street* provide the systematic instruction that students need to write. The following Grammar Transition Lessons and Practice Pages will supplement the core instruction with customized lessons that meet the particular needs of English language learners.

Each group of grammar lessons covers a topic, such as Nouns, Verbs, or Sentences. Each lesson is supported by a reproducible Practice Page that provides strong context for the skill. Throughout the Grammar Transition Lessons, a **Transition to English** feature identifies challenges faced by English language learners, based on the grammar of their home languages, as well as language knowledge that can transfer to English. Each lesson also includes a **Grammar in Action** feature to reinforce the skill through active learning.

In addition to the Grammar Transition Lessons and Practice Pages, you can further support grammar instruction with routines such as the following:

- **Emphasize sentence meaning.** Encourage students to try to understand and convey ideas rather than focusing only on separate words. Build their knowledge by presenting many examples that show how English sentences communicate, including sentences that the students say or write.

- **Strengthen oral language skills.** Allow beginning English speakers to work with partners when completing grammar activities, talking about what English words and sentences mean. Encourage them to make up new phrases and sentences together.

- **Engage students as active learners.** Students who are acquiring English will make mistakes but need encouragement rather than constant correction. Let them take risks, communicate imperfectly, chant sentences, and have fun with English.

- **Relate to the home language.** Whenever possible, help students build on what they already know by making connections between a target grammar skill and the home language. Use available resources, such as bilingual staff members, bilingual dictionaries, language Web sites, and the students themselves, to gather information about the home language.

Transition to English

Common Nouns

In languages such as Spanish and French, nouns are masculine or feminine. You can point out that while some nouns in English refer to males or females (boy, girl, uncle, aunt), English nouns do not have masculine and feminine endings.

Grammar *in Action*

Noun Hunt Have partners look through picture books and make a list of nouns they find in the pictures or texts.

Transition to English

Proper Nouns

Students who are literate in nonalphabetic languages such as Chinese, Korean, and Japanese may not be familiar with capitalizing proper nouns.

Grammar *in Action*

Special People and Places On chart paper, have students draw pictures and write or dictate the names of people and places that are special to them. Remind them to use capital letters.

Common Nouns

Introduce Point to objects in the room, and have students name them. Tell students: *We have names for the things around us. A noun is a word that names something or somebody.*

Teach Present the concept and provide examples:
- A noun names a person, a place, an animal, or a thing.

person	place	animal	things
girl	yard	dog	box, music

Practice/Assess Copy and distribute page 68. Read the directions aloud, and name the items in the picture before students complete the page. (See answers on page 126.)

Proper Nouns

Special Names

Introduce Have students practice writing each other's names. Point out that each child's name begins with a capital letter. Tell students: *Each of us has our own special name. A proper noun is the special name of a person, place, animal, or thing. Proper nouns begin with capital letters.*

Teach Present the concept and provide examples:
- A proper noun names a special person, place, animal, or thing.
- A proper noun begins with a capital letter.

special person	special place	special animal	special thing
Sandra	Africa	Fifi	Statue of Liberty

Practice/Assess Copy and distribute page 69. Read the directions aloud. Help students name the people and animals in the picture before they complete the page. (See answers on page 126.)

© Pearson Education, Inc.

Titles and Abbreviations

Introduce Write the names of various school staff members on the board, including titles such as *Mr.*, *Mrs.*, and *Dr.* Read the names aloud with students, and underline the titles as you say them. Point out the titles that are abbreviations, or shortened forms of words.

Teach Present the concept and provide examples:
- Proper names may begin with a title such as *Mrs.* or *Dr.*
- A title begins with a capital letter. If a title is an abbreviation, it ends with a period.

Title	Example
Mr. *(mister)*	Mr. Garza
Ms. *(miz)*	Ms. Prince
Mrs. *(missus)*	Mrs. Dexter
Miss *(miss)*	Miss Wong
Dr. *(doctor)*	Dr. Marco

Practice/Assess Copy and distribute page 70. Read the directions aloud before students complete the page. (See answers on page 126.) Have students read their own answers aloud.

Days, Months, and Holidays

Introduce Ask students to name today's day and date. Write them on the board, and point out that the day and month begin with capital letters.

Teach Present the concept and provide examples:
- The names of the days of the week, months of the year, and holidays begin with capital letters.

Days of the Week	Months of the Year		Holidays (Examples)
Sunday	January	July	Memorial Day
Monday	February	August	Labor Day
Tuesday	March	September	Thanksgiving
Wednesday	April	October	
Thursday	May	November	
Friday	June	December	
Saturday			

Practice/Assess Copy and distribute page 71. Read the directions aloud. Go through the sample calendar with students before they complete the page. (See answers on page 126.)

Transition to English

Titles
- Students may not realize that, in English, the title *Doctor* is used for both men and women.
- In some countries, the word *Teacher* is used as a title. Point out that in the U.S. teachers are addressed with a title such as *Mr.*, *Mrs.*, or *Ms.*

Grammar *in Action*

Introductions Have students practice introducing adult staff members to each other, using the correct titles.

Transition to English

Days and Months
- In languages including Spanish, French, Polish, and Vietnamese, the names of days and months are not usually capitalized.
- In languages such as Chinese, Vietnamese, and Portuguese, the names of the days are formed by counting from the first day of the week.

Grammar *in Action*

Word Origins Have students use dictionaries that show etymologies to find out the origins of the English names for days of the week.

© Pearson Education, Inc.

Transition to English

Plural Nouns
- Spanish speakers use -s and -es endings for nouns.
- In some languages, including Chinese, Hmong, and Vietnamese, nouns do not have plural forms. Instead, the plural is indicated with an adjective.

Grammar *in Action*

Noun Sort Have students make a 3-column chart with the headings "add -s," "add -es," and "change y to i and add -es." Invite students to look through magazines to find nouns that fit each category

Transition to English

Irregular Plurals
English learners may add -s to irregular nouns in sentences or to nouns for which English uses the singular for a quantity: *sheeps, mens, clothings.*

Grammar *in Action*

Concentration Have partners create "singular noun" word cards: *child, tooth, leaf, foot, man,* and "irregular plural noun" cards, including incorrect forms: *childs, children, teeth, tooths, leafs, leaves, feet, feets, men, mans.* Partners place the "singular" and "plural" cards face down in two separate groups, then take turns drawing correct pairs.

Singular and Plural Nouns

Introduce Point to one book and say: *book.* Point to two books and say: *books.* Repeat with *(lunch)box* and *(lunch)boxes.* Have students name other singular and plural nouns as you point to them. Say: *A singular noun names one thing. A plural noun names more than one thing.* Plural *means "more than one."*

Teach Present the concept and provide examples:
- Add -s to most nouns to form the plural.
- If the noun ends in -ch, -sh, -s, -ss, or -x, add -es.
- If the noun ends in a consonant + y, change the y to i and add -es.

Add -s	Add -es	Change y → i and add -es
girl/girls	box/boxes	berry/berries

Practice/Assess Copy and distribute page 72 after teaching *Irregular Plural Nouns.*

Irregular Plural Nouns

Introduce Write this sentence on the board: The <u>children</u> brushed their <u>teeth.</u> Ask a volunteer to name the singular of the underlined nouns *(child, tooth).* Tell students: *Most nouns add -s or -es to form the plural. Some nouns form the plural in a special way. They are called* irregular plural nouns.

Teach Present the concept and provide examples:
- Most nouns add -s or -es: *books, girls, boxes, brushes.*
- Irregular plural nouns have special forms. Here are some examples:

Irregular Plural Nouns			
child/children	foot/feet	life/lives	man/men
ox/oxen	tooth/teeth	leaf/leaves	woman/women

Practice/Assess Copy and distribute page 72. Help students name the singular and plural nouns in the picture. (See answers on page 126.) Have students name the irregular plural nouns. As an extension, have students list the singular of the plural nouns.

© Pearson Education, Inc.

Singular Possessive Nouns

Introduce Display these sentences, gesturing as appropriate: *This is <u>Maya</u>. This is <u>Maya's</u> desk.* Explain: *The first sentence is about Maya. The second sentence says that Maya has something. To show that a person, place, or thing has or owns something, add an apostrophe* (point to apostrophe) *and the letter* s. *The word Maya's is called a* singular possessive noun.

Teach Present the concept and provide examples:
• A singular possessive noun ends in *'s*.

Singular Nouns	Singular Possessive Nouns	Examples
Sam	Sam's	Sam's mom
friend	friend's	friend's house
class	class's	class's pet
child	child's	child's jacket

Practice/Assess Copy and distribute page 73 after teaching *Plural Possessive Nouns*.

Plural Possessive Nouns

Introduce Display these sentences: *All my <u>students</u> have desks. These are my <u>students'</u> desks.* Encourage students to discuss the meaning of the two sentences. Explain: *To show that two or more people, places, or things have or own something, use a plural possessive noun.*

Teach Present the concept and provide examples:
• If the plural noun ends in *-s*, *-es*, or *-ies*, add an apostrophe (')
to make it possessive.
• If the plural noun does **not** end in *-s*, *-es*, or *-ies*, add *'s* to make it possessive.

Plural Nouns	Plural Possessive	Examples
friends	friends'	friends' houses
classes	classes'	classes' teachers
puppies	puppies'	puppies' tails
children	children's	children's jackets

Practice/Assess Copy and distribute page 73. Make sure students understand the directions. Have students read their completed sentences aloud. (See answers on page 126.)

ELL and Transition Handbook

Transition to English

Possessive Nouns
In many languages, speakers show possession in phrases rather than noun endings. Show students how to change phrases such as *the tail of the cat* and *the nest of the bird* to *the cat's tail* and *the bird's nest*, in order to show possession in English.

Grammar *in Action*

My Friend's Things Have students place school supplies on their desks. Then have students point to and name a friend's things. For example: *This is Lin's book. This is Lin's calculator.*

Transition to English

Plural Possessive Nouns
An apostrophe after the letter s may seem incorrect to many students. Explain the difference between clear examples such as *a cat's tail* and *cats' tails* or *a bird's nest* and *birds' nests*. Use pictures or simple drawings to help students understand.

Grammar *in Action*

In Other Words Provide sentences such as these, and ask students to rewrite or rephrase them using plural possessive nouns: *This cake belongs to the students. (This is the students' cake.) These chairs belong to the children. (These are the children's chairs.)*

Name _____

Common Nouns

Practice

- **Look** at the picture.
- **Name** the people, places, animals, and things in the picture.

People	Places	Animals	Things
girl	pond	bird	slide

Assess

- **Look** around the room. What do you see?
- **Write** six nouns. **Name** things that you see.

_____

_____

Name _____

Special Names

Practice

- **Look** at the picture.
- **Find** the children, animals, and places that have special names.
- **Write** the names. Remember to begin the names with a capital letter.

Names of Children	Names of Animals	Names of Places
Maya		

Assess

- Write the names of two people you know.

_____

- Write the names of two special places you know.

_____

Name _____

Titles and Abbreviations

Practice

- **Look** at the pictures.
- **Write** the name of each person.
- **Include** a title for each person.

Title	Use with:
Mr.	a man
Ms.	a woman
Mrs.	a married woman
Miss	an unmarried girl or woman
Dr.	a doctor (male or female)

Mark Tanaka

Mr. Turner

Eva Santos
8 p.m.
Tonight!

Eva Santos

Lisa Johnson

1. Who is the teacher? _____

2. Who is the doctor? _____

3. Who is the dancer? _____

4. Who is the carpenter? _____

Assess

- Write the names of four adults you know. Include their titles.

_____

_____

Name _____

Days, Months, and Holidays

Practice

- Use this class calendar to **answer** the questions.
- Remember to **begin** the names of days, months, and holidays with capital letters.

November

Sunday	Monday	Tuesday	Wednesday	Thursday	Friday	Saturday
				1	2	3
4	5	6 Election Day	7 LIBRARY VISIT	8	9	10
11 Veterans Day	12	13	14 LIBRARY VISIT	15	16	17
18	19	20	21 LIBRARY VISIT	22 Thanksgiving	23	24
25	26	27	28 LIBRARY VISIT	29	30 BOOK FAIR	

1. What holiday is on Thursday, November 22? _____

2. What holiday is on Sunday, November 11? _____

3. When is the Book Fair? _____

4. When is Election Day? _____

5. When does the class visit the library? _____

Assess

- **Write** the names of the seven days of the week.

_____

- **Write** the name of a holiday or another day that is important to you. **Tell the date** of the holiday, or when it takes place.

_____   _____
           Name of the holiday   Date of the holiday

Singular and Plural Nouns

Practice

- **Look** at the picture.
- **Write** three singular nouns. **Write** three plural nouns.

Singular Nouns	Plural Nouns
tree	flowers

Assess

- **Look** around the room. What do you see?
- **Write** three singular nouns and three plural nouns.

_____

_____

Name _____

Singular and Plural Possessive Nouns

Practice

- **Look** at the picture. **Read** the sentences.
- **Circle** the correct possessive noun to complete each sentence.

1. (Today, Today's) date is May 19.
2. It is time for the (childrens', children's) story hour.
3. The (reader's, readers) name is Ed.
4. The (lady's, ladies') book club chooses a book.

Assess

- Choose a singular possessive noun from the sentences above. Use it in another sentence here.

_____

- Choose a plural possessive noun from the sentences above. Use it in another sentence here.

_____

Verbs

Transition to English

Present Tense

English verb endings are simpler than verb endings in languages such as Spanish and Polish, which use different endings for person and number. However, students may need practice adding *-s* or *-es* to present-tense verbs with third-person singular subjects.

Grammar *in Action*

Present Tense Practice
Write these subjects on index cards: *The baby, The girls, Sam, My brother, I.* Write these verbs on another set: *work, sleep, jump, run, play.* Have students draw a card from each set and create a sentence.

Verbs in Present Tense

Introduce Perform these actions as you narrate: *I walk to the front of the room. I point to the board. The words* walk *and* point *are verbs. The tense of a verb tells when something happens. A verb in present tense, like* walk *or* point, *tells what happens now. To talk about one other person or thing, add* -s: He walks. She points.

Teach Present the concept and provide examples:
• Verbs in present tense tell what happens now.

	Verb	Example
I, you, we, they	see	I <u>see</u> my sister.
he, she, it	sees	She <u>sees</u> me.

Practice/Assess Copy and distribute page 79. Help students describe the picture. (See answers on page 126.)

Transition to English

Past Tense
• Explain that regular past-tense verbs in English always have an *-ed* ending.
• In Chinese, Hmong, and Vietnamese, verbs do not change to show the tense. Adverbs or expressions of time indicate when an action has taken place.

Grammar *in Action*

Make It Past Display a list of verbs: *walk, play, jump, call, move, push, listen, watch.* Begin to tell a story: *Yesterday I walked to the park with my friend.* Have students add to the story, using the verbs from the list in the past tense.

Verbs in Past Tense

Introduce Display these sentences: *I <u>walked</u> to the front of the room. I <u>pointed</u> to the board.* Explain: *I did these things in the past. Many verbs in past tense end with* -ed. *If a verb ends in* e, *like* move, *drop the* e *and then add* -ed: moved. *If a verb has one syllable and ends with a vowel followed by a consonant, such as* shop, *double the consonant before adding* -ed: shopped.

Teach Present the concept and provide examples:
• Verbs in past tense tell what happened in the past.

	Verbs in Past Tense
Add *-ed*	He <u>jumped</u> over the chair.
Drop the final *e* and add *-ed*	I <u>moved</u> the chair.
Double the consonant and add *-ed*	He <u>slipped</u> on the rug.

Practice/Assess Copy and distribute page 80 after teaching *Irregular Verbs,* page 75.

Irregular Verbs

Introduce Display these sentences: *I _think_ about you. I _write_ you a note. I _thought_ about you. I _wrote_ you a note.* Explain: *Usually, you add -ed to a verb to form the past tense. But here, I didn't use* thinked *or* writed. *Some verbs are not regular verbs. They are called* irregular verbs. *An irregular verb has a different spelling in the past tense.*

Teach Present the concept and provide examples:
• Irregular verbs do not add *-ed* to form the past tense.
• Irregular verbs have different spellings in the past tense.

Irregular Verbs	Past Tense
write	I _wrote_ a poem yesterday.
sing	I _sang_ a song last night.
eat	I _ate_ an apple earlier today.

Practice/Assess Copy and distribute page 80. Explain that some answers will be irregular verbs. (See answers on page 126.)

Transition to English

Irregular Verbs
Many English learners need extra practice with the variety of irregular verbs that also feature unfamiliar phonics elements, such as *catch/caught, buy/bought,* and *can/could.*

Grammar *in Action*

Double-sided Verbs
Prepare index cards with irregular verbs. On one side, write the present tense. On the other side, write the past tense: *write/wrote; sing/sang; make/made; give/gave; eat/ate; have/had.* Have partners dictate sentences to each other using the words on both sides.

Verbs in Future Tense

Introduce Say: *What will I do after school today? I _will go_ home. I _will eat_ a snack. I _will read_ my e-mail.* Explain: *To talk about the future, we use verbs in future tense. The future may be later today, next week, or even next year.* Write one of the statements and point out the word *will.* Say: *Use the helping verb* will *to form the future tense.*

Teach Present the concept and provide examples:
• Verbs in future tense tell what will happen in the future.

Verbs in Future Tense
I _will go_ home.
I _will eat_ a snack.
I _will do_ my homework.

Practice/Assess Copy and distribute page 81. Help students describe the picture. Review the meanings of the verbs. (See answers on page 126.)

Transition to English

Future Tense
Spanish, Haitian Creole, and Hmong speakers may use present tense in places where English calls for future tense. Help students practice verbs in statements such as *I will read later* and *After we hear the story, we will write a new story.*

Grammar *in Action*

What will you do? Have partners tell each other what they will do when they get home from school or at some other time. If students can pantomime the action, have them act out the verb.

Verbs

Transition to English

Verb Tenses

Speakers of several languages, including Arabic, may find the English distinction between the past and present perfect tenses unfamiliar. Show contrasting examples, and explain how the sense of time differs.

Grammar *in Action*

Present Participle Practice

Say and display these verbs: *jump, walk, talk, wave, laugh.* Have students give the present participle of each verb, with the subjects *I, you, she,* and *they.* Have them pantomime the actions and point to the corresponding subject.

Transition to English

Learning Verb Forms

Spanish, like English, has irregular verbs (such as *ser,* which means "to be," and *ir,* "to go"). Challenge students who are literate in Spanish to identify irregular Spanish verbs, and see whether English verbs with the same meanings are irregular.

Grammar *in Action*

Find the Parts Write the principal parts of *go, sing, take,* and *write* on index cards. Give each student a card. Students circulate to find others with principal parts of the same verb.

Principal Parts of Regular Verbs

Introduce Display these sentences: *I talk to you. I am talking to you. I talked to you. I have talked to you many times.* Explain: *A verb's tenses are made from four basic forms: Present, Present Participle, Past, and Past Participle. These are called the verb's* **principal parts**. *The present form is used in the first sentence. The second sentence uses the present participle form. The third sentence uses the past form, which is the -ed form of the regular verb. The fourth sentence uses the past participle.*

Teach Present the concept and provide examples:
- The four basic forms are called the principal parts.
- The present participle can use *am, is,* or *are* and the *-ing* form.
- The past participle uses *has, have,* or *had* and the *-ed* form.

	Principal Parts: Regular Verbs
Present	The baby plays all day.
Present Participle	The baby is playing now.
Past	You helped me yesterday.
Past Participle	You have helped me before.

Practice/Assess Copy and distribute page 82. Have students share their sentences. (See answers on page 126.)

Principal Parts of Irregular Verbs

Introduce Display these sentences: *You grow every day. You are growing so much! You grew an inch last year. You have grown an inch every year.* Point out the past and past participle: *Irregular verbs change spelling in these forms.*

Teach Present the concept and provide examples:
- The principal parts of irregular verbs are the same four kinds as the principal parts of regular verbs. The *-ing* form is made the same way, such as *growing* or *going.*
- But irregular verbs do not use the *-ed* ending for the past and the past participle. For example, we do not say "growed"; we say "grew." We do not say "have growed"; we say "have grown."

I go. I am going. I went. I have gone.
He sees it. He is seeing it. He saw it. He has seen it.

Practice/Assess Copy and distribute page 83. Remind students that irregular verbs have their own spellings of the past and past participle. (See answers on page 127.)

© Pearson Education, Inc.

Helping Verbs

Introduce Display these sentences: *I am planting seeds. They will grow fast. I have planted seeds before.* Explain: *The underlined parts are called* verb phrases. *The main verbs—planting, grow, and planted—show action. The helping verbs—am, will, and have—tell more about the action. The helping verb am tells what I am doing now. Will tells what the seeds will do in the future. Have tells what I have done that started in the past.*

Teach Present the concept and provide examples:
• Helping verbs can tell the time of the action.

	Helping Verbs
Present	The dog **is** wagging his tail.
Past	He **was** barking last night.
Future	He **will** stay inside tonight.
Started in the Past	You **have** helped me before.

Practice/Assess Copy and distribute page 84. Have students read their sentences aloud. (See answers on page 127.)

Transition to English

Helping Verbs
The uses of *have* and *had* as helping verbs may be familiar to Spanish-speaking students once they learn the English words. The Spanish verb *haber* is used similarly.

Grammar *in Action*

Time to Listen Have each student create three index cards labeled *present, past,* and *future.* Say these sentences and have students hold up the corresponding card: *You were playing basketball yesterday. You are listening to me now. You will go to the library later.* Encourage students to say other sentences with helping verbs.

Linking Verbs

Introduce Display these sentences: *I am tired. I feel sick. She seems sad. He is the leader. The car was new.* Explain: *In these sentences, the underlined words are called* linking verbs. *They tell what the subject is or what the subject is like.*

Teach Present the concept and provide examples:
• Linking verbs do not show actions.
• They tell what the subject is or what the subject is like.

Linking Verbs	**Examples**
is	Summer <u>is</u> here.
are	The days <u>are</u> longer.
feels	The sun <u>feels</u> warmer.

Practice/Assess Copy and distribute page 85. Help students describe what is happening in the picture. (See answers on page 127.)

Transition to English

Linking Verbs
• In languages including Chinese and Korean, linking verbs often are not required: *She tired. They sad.* Help students practice English sentences with linking verbs.
• Vietnamese speakers may use the English verb *have* in place of *There are* or *is,* as in "Inside the box have a gift." Help students practice with sentences using forms of *be.*

Grammar *in Action*

You Are My Friend Have partners tell each other three nice things they observe about each other: *You seem happy. You are smart. You are funny.*

Verbs

Transition to English

Contractions

Ask students if there are contractions in their home languages. (In Spanish, *a + el = al* and *de + el = del*; in Portuguese, *de + as = das*.) Explain that an English contraction uses an apostrophe to replace the missing letters.

Grammar *in Action*

Contraction Substitution
Say these sentences, and have students rephrase them using contractions: *You are hiding. I do not see you. I am going to find you. I will not stop looking.* If necessary, help students learn *you're, don't, I'm,* and *won't.*

Contractions

Introduce Display these sentences: *You're calling me. I'm far away. I can't hear you.* Explain: *The underlined words are contractions. A contraction is a shortened form of two words. An apostrophe* (point to an apostrophe) *takes the place of one or more letters. Look at these contractions:* you and are become you're. I and am become I'm. can and not become can't.

Teach Present the concept and provide examples:
- A contraction is a shortened form of two words.
- An apostrophe takes the place of a letter or letters that are removed when you write a contraction.

	Contractions
I *and* have	I've eaten breakfast.
Should *and* not	You shouldn't run in the hall.
Can *and* not	She can't come to my party.

Practice/Assess Copy and distribute page 86 after teaching *Negatives.*

Transition to English

Negatives

In Spanish, Haitian Creole, and some other languages, double negatives (similar to *We did not do nothing*) are correct. Tell students that standard English does not use double negatives.

Grammar *in Action*

Double Negatives Write these sentences on the board. Invite students to come up and show how they would fix the double negative. Ask them to read the new sentence. *I can't never tell you. I won't say nothing. I don't want nobody to hear.*

Negatives

Introduce Display these sentences: *I never eat fish. I don't ever eat fish.* Explain: *The underlined words are negatives. They mean "no" or "not." Contractions with* n't *are negatives. In English, we use only one negative with one verb.* I don't never eat fish *has a double negative. Take away one negative.* (See the first two examples.)

Teach Present the concept and provide examples:
- Use only one negative with one verb.
- Use a positive word in a sentence with *not.*

	Examples
Negative	Nothing is on the table.
Positive	I don't see anything there.
Negative	They went nowhere.
Positive	We didn't go anywhere.

Practice/Assess Copy and distribute page 86. Remind students to watch for double negatives. (See answers on page 127.)

Verbs in Present Tense

Practice

- **Look** at the picture. **Read** the sentences.
- **Write** the correct verb in present tense to complete each sentence.

bench

1. At 8:00, we _____ (wait, waits) for the bus.

2. Liz _____ (talk, talks) to her mom.

3. Adam _____ (sit, sits) on the bench.

4. I _____ (see, sees) the bus!

Assess

- **Look** at the picture. **Write** a sentence about the dog. Use a verb in present tense.

_____

Verbs in Past Tense

Practice

- **Look** at the picture. **Read** the sentences.
- **Circle** the correct verb in past tense.

toy dog → cake

Yesterday was my little sister's birthday. We (celebrated, celebrates) with a little party.

I (gived, gave) her a toy dog. She (play, played) with it all day. My mom (maked, made)

a chocolate cake. We (haved, had) a good time!

Assess

- **Look** at the picture again. **Write** another sentence about the party. Use the verb *ate*.

_____

Name _____

Verbs in Future Tense

Practice

- **Look** at the picture. **Read** the story. **Read** the verbs in the box.
- **Write** the correct verb in future tense to complete each sentence.

The mother bird _____ food for the babies.

In a few days, she _____ them to fly. Soon,

the baby birds _____ big and strong. They

_____ away from the nest.

will find	will fly	will teach	will grow

Assess

- What do you think the mother bird will do when the baby birds fly away? **Write** a sentence about it.

_____

Name _____

Principal Parts of Regular Verbs

Practice

- **Look** at the picture. **Read** the sentences.
- **Circle** the verb in each sentence. **Write** *present*, *present participle*, *past*, or *past participle* to name the principal part of the verb.

1. The concert has started. _____

2. We listen to Sofia, Ben, and Ray. _____

3. Sofia and Ben are playing violins. _____

4. Sofia has played the violin for three years. _____

5. Ray plays the flute well. _____

Assess

- **Write** a sentence about the concert. Use the present participle *playing*.

_____

_____

© Pearson Education, Inc.

Name _____

Principal Parts of Irregular Verbs

Practice

- **Look** at the picture. **Read** the sentences.
- **Circle** the verb in each sentence. **Write** *present*, *present participle*, *past*, or *past participle* to name the principal part of each irregular verb.

1. Yesterday I went to the doctor's office. _____

2. I go every year. _____

3. I have grown two inches this year. _____

4. I am growing very fast. _____

Assess

- **Write** a sentence to say what the doctor did. Use the past tense verb *wrote*.

_____

Name _____

Helping Verbs

Practice

- **Look** at the picture. **Read** the sentences.
- **Circle** the verb phrase in each sentence. **Underline** the helping verb.

1. We are learning about dolphins in class.

2. We have seen dolphins at the zoo.

3. I am using the Internet now.

4. I will give my report tomorrow.

Assess

- **Write** a sentence about the girl's report. Use the verb phrase *will tell*.

ELL and Transition Handbook

Linking Verbs

Practice

- **Look** at the picture. **Read** the sentences.
- **Circle** the linking verb in each sentence.

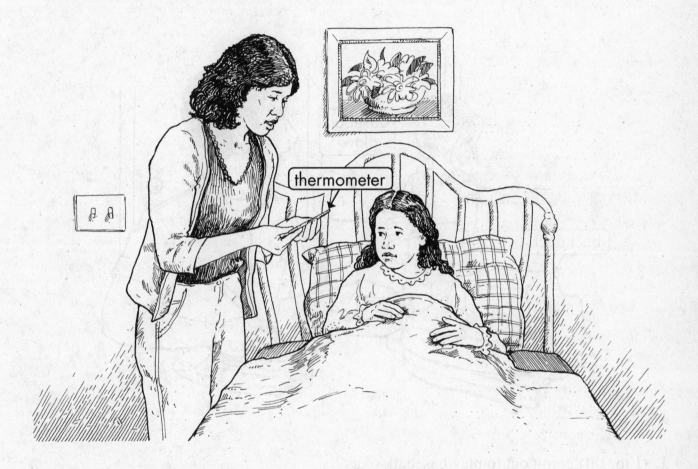

thermometer

1. I am sick today.

2. I feel tired and cold.

3. Mom seems worried.

4. My temperature is 102°.

Assess

- **Write** a sentence about the girl. Use the linking verb *is*.

Name _____

Contractions and Negatives

Practice

- **Look** at the picture. **Read** the sentences.
- **Circle** the correct word to complete each sentence.

1. (I'm, I'll) going out to play baseball, okay?

2. (Shouldn't, Should'nt) you do your homework first?

3. Oh, (I've, I'm) already done it.

4. (You're, Your) such a good student!

5. I won't (ever, never) neglect my schoolwork.

Assess

- **Write** a sentence about the girl's dad. Use a contraction with *not*.

_____

Subjects and Predicates

Introduce Display this sentence: _The girl walks to school._ Explain that "The girl" is the subject of the sentence. The sentence is about the girl. A sentence is about its subject. Explain that "walks to school" is the predicate. What does the girl do? (walks to school) A predicate tells something about the subject.

Teach Present the concept and provide examples:
- The subject of a sentence tells whom or what the sentence is about.
- The predicate of a sentence tells what the subject is or what the subject does.

Subject	Predicate
Sam	went to the store.
The students	write a paper.
The vegetables	are fresh.
My dog	had puppies.

Practice/Assess Copy and distribute page 94. Look at the picture after students complete the page. Have students contribute other sentences and identify the subjects and predicates. (See answers on page 127.)

Subject-Verb Agreement

Introduce Display these sentences: _The bird sings a song. The birds sing a song._ Encourage students to discuss the differences between the underlined parts. Explain: _The first sentence has a singular subject:_ bird. _The second sentence has a plural subject:_ birds. _The subject and the verb must work together, or agree. That's why the first sentence uses_ sings _and the second sentence uses_ sing.

Teach Present the general concept and provide examples:
- If the subject is singular, add -s to the verb.
- If the subject is plural, do not add -s to the verb.

Subject	Verb
man	dances
Mom	works
friends	play
both feet	hurt

Practice/Assess Copy and distribute page 95. Help students describe the picture, emphasizing subject-verb agreement. (See answers on page 127.)

Transition to English

Subjects and Predicates
The typical English sequence of subject then predicate is not standard in some languages. For example, in Spanish the verb often appears before the subject, while in Korean and Hindi the verb typically appears at the end of a sentence.

Grammar _in Action_

Sentence Scramble Write these sentences onto strips: _My friend rides a bike. My dog barks at cats. The fish smells good. The clown is funny._ Cut each strip into subject and predicate. Have students scramble the sentence parts to form new sentences such as _The fish rides a bike._

Transition to English

Verbs and Subjects
Students of various language backgrounds may add -s to both the nouns and verbs in sentences: _The robots walks._ Point out that, in English, verbs add -s for singular nouns (_A robot walks_), not for verbs with plural nouns (_The robots walk_).

Grammar _in Action_

News Headlines
Encourage students to scour the day's headlines for examples of subject-verb agreement. For example: _Sales Decline; Stocks Sink; Gas Prices Rise; Dog Saves Girl._

Transition to English

Word Order

- Help students see that word order strongly affects meaning in English. *Lee thanked Tony* has a different meaning from *Tony thanked Lee.*
- See the Transition note about the sequence of subjects and predicates on page 87.

Grammar *in Action*

Correct Order Say these groups of words: *The food is good. Is good the food. My friend rides a bike. Rides a bike my friend. Plays the dog. The dog plays.* Have students say which sentences are in correct word order.

Transition to English

Sentence Fragments

Spanish- and Chinese-speaking students may omit some pronouns as sentence subjects because in their home languages the pronoun may be unnecessary. For example, the Spanish equivalent of *Am reading* is a complete sentence.

Grammar *in Action*

Sentence or Fragment? Say these groups of words. Have students call out *sentence* or *fragment* after each one: *My brother. We walk to school. We ride on the bus. In the car. After school.* Invite students to contribute other sentences.

Word Order

Introduce Display these sentences and read them aloud, gesturing: *The bird flies. Flies the bird.* Ask: *What is the subject of the first sentence? (The bird) The second sentence does not sound right. The words are not in the right order to make a statement. In an English statement, the subject usually comes first. The predicate usually follows.*

Teach Present the concept and provide examples:
- Sentences need to have words in the right order.
- In a statement, the subject usually comes first. The predicate usually follows.

In the right order:	Pablo is my friend.
Not in the right order:	Is friend my Pablo.

Practice/Assess Copy and distribute page 96. Help students describe what is happening in the picture. (See answers on page 127.)

Complete Sentences and Sentence Fragments

Introduce Write this sentence and fragment on the board: *Tom went to the library. Went to the library.* Ask: *Who went to the library? (Tom) Which sentence tells you this? The first sentence tells a complete idea. It says who did something. The second set of words (went to the library) is called a sentence fragment. It does not tell a complete idea. It does not say who went to the library. How would you make this fragment a complete sentence? (Add a subject.)*

Teach Present the concept and provide examples:
- A sentence tells a complete idea.
- A fragment is a piece of a sentence. It does not tell a complete idea.

Sentence	Cheny eats her lunch.
Fragment	Her lunch in a bag.

Practice/Assess Copy and distribute page 97. As an extension, have students choose a fragment from the Practice and create a sentence from it. (See answers on page 127.)

Types of Sentences

Statements

Introduce Display these sentences: *I went to the library. My brother went too. We both found good books.* Say: *Let's look at these sentences. Each one starts with a capital letter and ends with a period. Each one tells something. A sentence that tells something is called a* statement.

Teach Present the concept and provide examples:
- A sentence that tells something is called a *statement*.
- It begins with a capital letter and ends with a period.

Statements
I had a party yesterday.
All of my friends came to my house.
You ate pizza.

Practice/Assess Copy and distribute page 98 after teaching *Questions*.

Questions

Introduce Display these sentences: *What is your name? Where do you live? How old are you? Do you have any brothers?* Ask: *How are these sentences different from statements? They each ask something, and they end with question marks. A sentence that asks something is called a* question. Model the difference in intonation between these two sentences: *That is your dog. Is that your dog?*

Teach Present the general concept and provide examples:
- A sentence that asks something is called a *question*.
- It starts with a capital letter and ends with a question mark.

Questions
How are you?
Did you go to Sam's party?
Does Ami like pizza?

Practice/Assess Copy and distribute page 98. Help students describe the picture. (See answers on page 127.)

Transition to English

Statements
Children who have begun to read in Spanish and other alphabetic languages may recognize that sentences begin with capital letters and end with periods.

Grammar *in Action*

Fix the Statements Write groups of words such as these on the board, including the mistakes: *my friends are funny. / They tell me jokes / I laugh every day* Have volunteers come up and fix the statements by adding correct punctuation and a capital letter at the beginning.

Transition to English

Questions
Speakers of Chinese, Vietnamese, and other Asian languages often form questions by adding words to statements, comparable to *The food is hot, no?* or *You see or not see the bird?* Provide model English questions for students to understand and to follow the patterns.

Grammar *in Action*

Twenty Questions Have pairs of students ask each other questions about what they did yesterday. For example, *What did we do in school yesterday? What is your favorite subject?*

`Transition to English`

Exclamations

Speakers of Russian, Polish, and other languages may need to practice correct word order in exclamations. Have students make and use sentence strips, correcting exclamations such as *We enjoy very much movies!*

Grammar *in Action*

Interjection Charades
Write these interjections on index cards: *Ouch! Wow! Oh, no! Hooray!* Display them. Have a volunteer secretly choose an interjection and pantomime a scene that would elicit that interjection. Whoever guesses correctly takes the next turn.

`Transition to English`

Commands

Vietnamese speakers may recognize commands when they include an adverb or another clue word: *Go to school now. Take this to the office; go now.*

Grammar *in Action*

Teddy Bear Teach students the jump rope chant "Teddy Bear," in which the jumper obeys these commands while jumping rope: *Teddy Bear, Teddy Bear, turn around. Teddy Bear, Teddy Bear, touch the ground. Teddy Bear, Teddy Bear, stomp your feet. Teddy Bear, Teddy Bear, show your teeth.* Invite students to play.

Exclamations and Interjections

Introduce Write and say in an excited voice: *I am so happy!* Have students repeat, and then ask: *What feeling does that sentence express? (excitement; happiness)* Whenever you say something with strong feeling, you are saying an exclamation. A written exclamation ends with an exclamation mark. Next, write and say: *Hooray!* Explain: *This word also shows strong feeling and ends in an exclamation mark. However, it is not a complete sentence. It is called an* interjection.

Teach Present the concept and provide examples:
- An exclamation is a sentence that shows strong feeling. It ends with an exclamation mark.
- An interjection is a word or group of words that shows strong feeling. It ends with an exclamation mark, but it is not a complete sentence.

Exclamation	I have a new baby brother!
Interjection	Wow!

Practice/Assess Copy and distribute page 99. Remind students that exclamations are complete sentences. (See answers on page 127.)

Commands

Introduce Give students various commands such as these: *Please stand up. Walk to the front of the class. Say hello. Sit down.* Ask: *How are these sentences the same? Sentences that tell someone to do something are called* commands.

Teach Present the concept and provide examples:
- A command is a sentence that tells someone to do something.
- It begins with a capital letter and ends with a period.

Commands
Open the door. Turn on the light. Sweep the floor.

Practice/Assess Copy and distribute page 100. Have students use it as a model for writing another recipe. (See answers on page 128.)

Simple and Compound Sentences

Introduce Display these sentences: *I went to Sal's house. We watched a movie.* Ask students to tell the subjects and predicates. Explain: *A simple sentence has one subject and one predicate. You can join the two simple sentences this way: I went to Sal's house, and we watched a movie. The new sentence is called a compound sentence. The two simple sentences are joined with the word and.*

Teach Present the concept and provide examples:
* A simple sentence has one subject and one predicate.
* A compound sentence has two simple sentences joined by a comma and one of these words: *and, but,* or *or.*

Simple Sentences	Lena is my sister. I love her. I like peanuts. They make me sick. You can walk to school. I can drive you.
Compound Sentences	Lena is my sister, and I love her. I like peanuts, but they make me sick. You can walk to school, or I can drive you.

Practice/Assess Copy and distribute page 101. In the first compound sentence, help students see the two simple sentences. (See answers on page 128.)

Combining Sentences

Introduce Display these sentences: *I ate a sandwich. I drank some milk.* Ask: *What is the subject of both sentences? You can combine two sentences that have the same subject: I ate a sandwich and drank some milk.* Display these sentences: *Max went to the beach. I went to the beach. What is the predicate of both sentences? You can combine two sentences that have the same predicate: Max and I went to the beach.*

Teach Present the concept and provide examples:
* Combine two sentences that have the same subject.
* Combine two sentences that have the same predicate.

Same Subject	Dan sat down. Dan did his homework. Dan sat down and did his homework.
Same Predicate	Miguel walked to school. I walked to school. Miguel and I walked to school.

Practice/Assess Copy and distribute page 102. Help students describe the picture. (See answers on page 128.)

Transition to English

Compound Sentences
Students may have difficulty distinguishing the clauses in a compound sentence in English. Give them additional practice finding the subject and verb within each independent clause.

Grammar *in Action*

Make a Compound Say several pairs of simple sentences. Have students say compound sentences, keeping in mind the differences among *and, but,* and *or: I want to buy juice. I do not have a dollar. / I can drink water. I can borrow a dollar. / Tom is my friend. He gave me a dollar.*

Transition to English

Combining Sentences
Speakers of Indonesian and some other Asian languages may need practice combining sentences.

Grammar *in Action*

Form Sentences Make a set of sentence cards: *Mari wrote a poem. David sings. Rita went home.* Make a second set and distribute: *Mari read it to the class. David plays the guitar. Simón went home.* Read a sentence from the first set. The student holding a sentence with the same subject or predicate reads it. Have a volunteer form a combined sentence.

Transition to English

Complex Sentences

Functional words such as *if, that, so,* and *because* are often used somewhat differently in English than how their equivalents are used in other languages. Help students practice and understand usages of these words.

Grammar *in Action*

Have students write these sentences and tell whether they are complex or not: *My sister's name is Lupe.* (no) *Since she is little, I help her with homework.* (yes) *I also tie her shoes.* (no) *When I was little, my mom helped me.* (yes)

Transition to English

Dependent Clauses

Provide models of dependent clauses that begin with words such as *after, although, as, because, before, if, since, then, until, when,* and *while.* These words may have uses that are unfamiliar to students of many language backgrounds.

Grammar *in Action*

Say these dependent clauses. Have students add independent clauses to form complex sentences: *Since I was little / When I grow up / Because it was raining / If you help me / Until my alarm clock rings.* Have students write the complex sentences.

Complex Sentences

Introduce Review compound sentences. Then present these complex sentences: <u>When I run</u>, I feel good. I feel good <u>when I run</u>. Explain: *This type of sentence is called a* complex sentence. *It has two parts, called* clauses. *The underlined part cannot stand alone as a sentence. If it comes first in the sentence, use a comma. The other part* (I feel good) *can stand alone as a complete sentence.*

Teach Present the concept and provide examples:
- A complex sentence is made of two clauses.
- The two clauses are joined together with words such as *because, when, since, if,* or *until.*

Complex Sentences	When I grow up, I will be a teacher. I will be a teacher when I grow up.

Practice/Assess Copy and distribute page 103. Remind students that a complex sentence has two clauses. (See answers on page 128.)

Independent and Dependent Clauses

Introduce Present this complex sentence: *We cross the street <u>when the light is green</u>.* Explain: *The underlined part cannot stand alone as a sentence. It is a* dependent clause. *It depends on another part. The other part* (we cross the street) *can stand alone. It is an* independent clause.

Teach Present the concept and provide examples:
- A complex sentence is made of an independent clause and a dependent clause.
- The dependent clause cannot stand alone.
- The independent clause can stand alone.

Independent Clause	Dependent Clause
I am happy	because I passed the test.

Practice/Assess Copy and distribute page 104. Remind students that dependent clauses often start with words such as *since, although, when, if,* or *until.* (See answers on page 128.)

Commas

In a Series and in Direct Address

Introduce Display this sentence: *My favorite colors are red, blue, and yellow.* Point out the commas. Say: *Commas help you understand a sentence. They tell you when to pause, or rest. Put commas after items in a series of words such as red, blue, and yellow.* Display these sentences: *Kim, may I use your pen? Yes, Lucas, you may.* Say: *When we write a sentence in which a person is directly addressed by name, we use a comma.*

Teach Present the concept and provide examples:
- Use commas to separate items in a series.
- Use commas with direct address.

Commas in a Series	I like baseball, basketball, and soccer. I play Monday, Wednesday, and Friday.
Commas in Direct Address	Lori, would you come here? Yes, Mom, I'm coming. I need your help, Lori.

Practice/Assess Copy and distribute page 105 after the lesson on commas with appositives and introductory phrases.

With Appositives and Introductory Phrases

Introduce Display these sentences: *Mr. Hays, <u>my teacher</u>, speaks Spanish. <u>Yes</u>, I know.* Explain: *The underlined part of the first sentence is called an appositive. It is a noun phrase that describes another noun. Use a comma before and after an appositive. The underlined part of the second sentence is called an introductory word. Put a comma after an introductory word or phrase such as* well, no, oh, *and "in other words."*

Teach Present the concept and provide examples:
- Use a comma before and after an appositive.
- Use a comma after an introductory word or phrase.

Appositives	Mr. Sims, <u>my neighbor</u>, has a dog. The dog, <u>a poodle</u>, barks all night.
Introductory Words or Phrases	<u>Oh</u>, I am very sorry. <u>In other words</u>, you cannot sleep.

Practice/Assess Copy and distribute page 105. Read the sentences, pausing where commas belong. (See answers on page 128.)

Transition to English

Commas
Some students may use commas in places where periods are used in the United States, such as in decimals (1,5 for 1.5). Determine the intended meaning, and clarify the standard usage in American English.

Grammar *in Action*

May I Take Your Order? On the board, write menu items such as *soup, salad, sandwich, milk, tea, juice.* Have pairs play the roles of server and customer at a café. The server starts with *"May I take your order?"* The customer names three items, such as: *I want soup, salad, and milk.* The server says and writes the order: *"He wants soup, salad, and milk."* Have students switch roles.

Transition to English

Commas
Commas can be challenging for any student. English language learners may need help distinguishing needs for commas from uses of other kinds of punctuation.

Grammar *in Action*

Comma Practice
Brainstorm names of school staff. Write their names and job titles, such as *Mrs. Olson, the bus driver.* Have students use this information to write sentences with appositives.

Name _____

Subjects and Predicates

Practice

- **Look** at the picture. **Read** the sentences.
- **Circle** the complete subject of each sentence. **Underline** the complete predicate of each sentence.

1. The farmer's market is a busy place.

2. The sun shines brightly today.

3. A man sells big, red tomatoes.

4. A woman puts carrots into her bag.

Assess

- **Look** at the picture again. **Write** a subject to begin this sentence.

_____ sells flowers at the market.

Subject-Verb Agreement

Practice

- **Look** at the picture. **Read** the sentences.
- **Circle** the correct verb to complete each sentence.

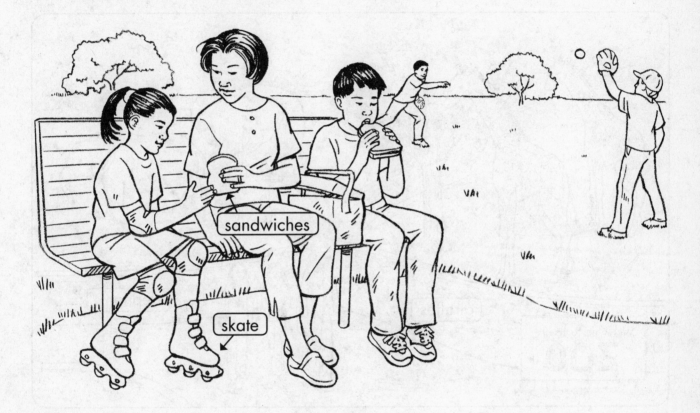

1. Mom (give, gives) the children sandwiches.

2. The children (enjoy, enjoys) a day at the park.

3. The boys (throw, throws) a ball.

4. The girl (like, likes) to skate.

Assess

- **Write** a sentence about one person or two persons doing something at the park. Make sure that the subject and the verb work together.

Word Order

Practice

- **Look** at the picture. **Read** the sentences.
- **Circle** the sentences with the words in the right order.

1. We went to the zoo.
   Went to the zoo we.

2. Elephants I saw the.
   I saw the elephants.

3. Were tall the giraffes.
   The giraffes were tall.

Assess

- **Look** at the picture again. **Write** another sentence about it.

Name _____

Complete Sentences and Sentence Fragments

Practice

- **Look** at the picture. **Read** the groups of words.
- **Write** each group of words that is a complete sentence.

1. How the baker bakes.   The baker bakes bread.

_____

2. He puts the bread into the oven.   Many different breads.

_____

3. Makes delicious and round pies.   He makes delicious pies.

_____

Assess

- Choose one of the fragments. Add more words and make a complete sentence.

_____

© Pearson Education, Inc.

Name _____

Statements and Questions

Practice

• **Look** at the picture. **Read** the sentences.
• **Write** each sentence correctly. If it is a statement, end it with a period. If it is a
  question, end it with a question mark.

1. This is Raquel's party

_____

2. Do you like to dance

_____

3. Raquel's mom takes pictures

_____

4. Len eats pizza

_____

5. What time is it

_____

Assess

• **Look** at the picture again. **Write** another question about Raquel's party. Start with
  one of these words: *did, was, when, how.*

_____

Name _____

Exclamations and Interjections

Practice

- **Look** at the picture. **Read** the sentences.
- **Write** the exclamation or interjection that each person says.

I am running fast!

Hooray! You will win!

I want to go home!

Assess

- What would you say if you won a contest? **Write** it here.

_____

© Pearson Education, Inc.

Name _____

Commands

Practice

- **Look** at the pictures. **Read** the sentences.
- **Circle** the sentences that are commands.

1. Lemonade is easy to make.

2. Squeeze lemon juice into the pitcher.

3. Add water, sugar, and ice.

4. This lemonade is so good!

Assess

- **Write** how to make lemonade. Use only commands. Use these words: *find, cut, squeeze, add.*

_____

_____

ELL and Transition Handbook

Name _____

Simple and Compound Sentences

Practice

- **Look** at the picture. **Read** the compound sentences.
- **Write** the two simple sentences in each compound sentence.

bowl of cereal

1. Mom needs to go to work, but Jon is still eating his cereal.

_____

_____

2. Jon needs to hurry, or Mom will be late for work.

_____

_____

3. Jon finishes his cereal, and they both run out the door.

_____

_____

Assess

- Do you think Jon's mom will be late for work? **Write** a compound sentence about it.

_____

_____

Name _____

Combining Sentences

Practice

- **Look** at the picture. **Read** the sentences.
- **Combine** each pair of sentences. Use the underlined words only once in the new sentence.

1. Dad <u>went to the park</u>. I <u>went to the park</u>.

_____

2. <u>Dad</u> sat on a bench. <u>Dad</u> read his book.

_____

3. <u>I</u> found a stick. <u>I</u> threw it.

_____

4. <u>My dog</u> ran far. <u>My dog</u> got the stick.

_____

Assess

- **Write** another sentence using one of the underlined parts.

_____

_____

Complex Sentences

Practice

- **Look** at the picture.
- **Read** the sentences. **Check** the circle next to the ones that are complex sentences.

1. ○ I watch Tran because she is a good painter.
   ○ She is making a big, beautiful painting!

2. ○ I want a painting for my room.
   ○ Since this painting is big, Tran will put it in Mom's room.

3. ○ Tran will make a smaller painting.
   ○ She will start it when she finishes this one.

Assess

- **Write** another complex sentence about the girl who is painting.

_____

_____

Name _____

Independent and Dependent Clauses

Practice

- **Look** at the picture. **Read** the sentences.
- **Circle** the dependent clause in each sentence.

basketball

1. After I do my homework, I play basketball.

2. When David is there, he plays with me.

3. We play until we are very tired.

4. David goes home because he has homework.

Assess

- **Write** a sentence that starts with *When David goes home.*

_____

_____

Commas

Practice

- **Look** at the picture.
- **Read** the sentences. **Add** commas where they are needed.

1. Gino's the new Italian restaurant has great food.

2. Mom thank you for buying us dinner.

3. I want soup salad pizza and lemonade.

4. Well I hope you can eat all that!

Assess

- **Write** three things you would order at your favorite restaurant. Then read your sentence to a partner. Remember to pause after each comma.

_____

_____

Pronouns

Transition to English

Subject Pronouns
- In Spanish, unlike English, speakers may omit subject pronouns because Spanish verbs can indicate the subjects.
- Korean speakers may add a subject pronoun after the noun, reflecting a pattern in Korean: *Nathan, he is my brother.*

Grammar *in Action*

In the Classroom Say these sentences, and have students rephrase them using subject pronouns: <u>Ana</u> sits in the third row. <u>Max</u> sits here. <u>Ana and Max</u> are cousins. <u>The sandwich</u> is the teacher's lunch.

Subject Pronouns

Introduce Point to yourself and say *I am a teacher.* Point to the students and say *You are students.* Point to a boy and say *He is a student.* Point to a girl and say *She is a student.* Indicate everyone in the room and say *We are at school.* Explain: *Pronouns such as* I, you, he, she, we, *and* they *are used in place of nouns or noun phrases such as people's names. These pronouns are used for subjects of sentences. We do not say* Me am a teacher *or* Him is a student.

Teach Present the concept and provide examples:
- A subject pronoun is used as the subject of a sentence.

	Subject Pronouns
Singular	I, you, he, she, it
Plural	we, you, they

Practice/Assess Copy and distribute page 109. Review gender and number of subject pronouns. (See answers on page 128.)

Transition to English

Object Pronouns
Spanish, Chinese, and Vietnamese speakers and other English learners may use subject pronouns as objects *(Give the book to she.)* until practice in English clarifies the different pronoun forms.

Grammar *in Action*

Finish the Sentence
Pose open-ended sentences, cueing object pronoun endings by gesturing to different people in the room: *I will help...* [gesture toward a girl] Students should finish the sentence: *her.*

Object Pronouns

Introduce Display these sentences: *Give the book to <u>me</u>. Mom made <u>us</u> a snack. They talked with <u>Tom and her</u>.* Explain: *Pronouns such as* me, you, him, her, us, *and* them *are used after verbs, or after words such as* for, at, with, *or* to. *We do not say* Give the book to I *or* Mom made we a snack.

Teach Present the concept and provide examples:
- An object pronoun is used in the predicate, after an action verb or preposition.

	Object Pronouns
Singular	me, you, him, her, it
Plural	us, you, them

Practice/Assess Copy and distribute page 110. Help students describe the picture. (See answers on page 128.)

© Pearson Education, Inc.

Possessive Pronouns

Introduce Hold a book and say: *This is my book. This book is mine.* Explain: *The words* my *and* mine *are possessive pronouns. They show that I have this book. Possessive pronouns show who or what has or owns something.*

Teach Present the concept and provide examples:
- Use *my, your, her, our,* and *their* before nouns.
- Use *mine, yours, hers, ours,* and *theirs* alone.
- *His* and *its* can be used before nouns and alone.

Possessive Pronouns
Before nouns: This is <u>your</u> pen. It is <u>her</u> doll.
Alone: The shoes are <u>mine</u>. The doll is <u>hers</u>.
Both: The pen is <u>his</u>. This is <u>his</u> home.

Practice/Assess Copy and distribute page 111. Have students read their sentences aloud. (See answers on page 128.)

Transition to English

Possessive Pronouns
Asian-language students and others may try various forms for possessive pronouns—*the hat of her, you hat*—or may not always state the pronoun (*Mo Yun took off hat*). Provide practice with possessive pronouns.

Grammar *in Action*

Around the Room Have students look around the room and identify objects that belong to them or to someone else. Have them use each item in a sentence with a possessive pronoun: *Here is my pencil. This calculator is yours.*

Pronouns and Antecedents

Introduce Display these sentences: <u>Sam</u> says <u>he</u> will go. Explain: *In this sentence, the pronoun* he *replaces the name* Sam. *The sentence does not have to say, "Sam says Sam will go." Sam, the noun being replaced, is called the* antecedent. *A pronoun must agree in number and gender with the noun or noun phrase it replaces. Sam is one person, a boy. So we use the pronoun* he, *which is singular and masculine. The pronoun for a girl is feminine:* she. <u>Lisa</u> says <u>she</u> will go.

Teach Present the concept and provide examples:
- A pronoun and its antecedent must agree in number and gender.

Pronouns and Antecedents
<u>Laura</u> knows what <u>she</u> wants.
<u>Bobi and Ben</u> call me when <u>they</u> get home.
<u>The parrot</u> repeats what <u>it</u> hears.

Practice/Assess Copy and distribute page 112. Remind students that singular antecedents are either masculine, feminine, or neuter. (See answers on page 129.)

Transition to English

Third-Person Pronouns
Some Asian languages emphasize distinctions such as older and younger people rather than gender pronouns. At first, students may use pronouns that do not match the antecedents—*Joanne and his family; throw the ball to it* (rather than *him*).

Grammar *in Action*

Antecedent Agreement
Display this sentence: <u>The cat</u> eats what <u>it</u> likes. Write the following on cards and distribute to students: *The girl; My brother; The children; The teacher; she; he; they.* Invite students to substitute antecedents and pronouns in the sentence using the cards.

Pronouns

Transition to English

Indefinite Pronouns
In some languages, the words that mean *everyone* and *everybody* are plural. Students may try using verbs such as "Everyone are" or "Everybody say. . . ."

Grammar *in Action*

Everyone in Concert
Show students a picture of a concert. Have them describe it, using these or similar starter sentences: *Everyone is in the concert. Some are singers.*

Indefinite Pronouns

Introduce Display this sentence: <u>Someone</u> wrote you a note. Ask: *Who is this someone? If we don't know, then we can use an indefinite pronoun:* someone. *Other singular indefinite pronouns are:* anybody, everyone, everything, either, each. *Some plural indefinite pronouns are:* few, several, both, others, many, all, some.

Teach Present the concept and provide examples:
• Indefinite pronouns may not refer to specific nouns.
• Use the correct verb forms with singular indefinite pronouns and with plural indefinite pronouns.

	Indefinite Pronouns
Singular	<u>Everyone</u> is clapping. <u>Somebody</u> has sung very well.
Plural	<u>Some</u> are standing. <u>Others</u> are sitting.

Practice/Assess Copy and distribute page 113 after teaching *Reflexive Pronouns.*

Transition to English

Reflexive Pronouns
Chinese speakers learning English may omit a second reference to one person in a sentence. Rather than "I enjoyed myself," a student may feel that "I enjoyed" is complete.

Grammar *in Action*

Pronoun Match Write these subject pronouns on index cards: *I, you, he, she, it, we, they.* Make another set with reflexive pronouns. Have students draw a card from the reflexive set and match it to its subject pronoun.

Reflexive Pronouns

Introduce Display these sentences: *I will write a note to <u>myself</u>. She will buy <u>herself</u> a snack. Explain:* Myself *and* herself *are reflexive pronouns.*

Teach Present the concept and provide examples:
• Reflexive pronouns reflect the action back on the subject: *They gave themselves a chance to rest.*
• Reflexive pronouns end in *-self* or *-selves.*

	Reflexive Pronouns
Singular	himself, herself, myself, itself, yourself
Plural	ourselves, yourselves, themselves

Practice/Assess Copy and distribute page 113. Have students read the completed sentences aloud. (See answers on page 129.)

© Pearson Education, Inc.

Name _____

Subject Pronouns

Practice

- **Look** at the picture. **Read** each sentence.
- **Circle** the correct pronoun in parentheses.

1. David and (I, me) are good friends.

2. (Us, We) ride the bus together every morning.

3. Today there were many cars. (Them, They) moved very slowly.

4. The bus driver had a phone, so (she, her) called the school.

Assess

- **Write** a sentence about the students on the bus. Start with the subject pronoun *They*.

Object Pronouns

Practice

- **Look** at the picture. **Read** the sentences.
- **Circle** the correct pronoun to complete each sentence.

The Spanish Club is having a bake sale. Mrs. Ruiz asked Jen and (me, I) to bake

something. Many students bought cookies from (we, us). I had fun baking

(them, they). How many cookies are left? I will count (it, them).

Assess

- **Write** another sentence about the bake sale. Use *him* or *her*.

_____

Name _____

Possessive Pronouns

Practice

- **Look** at the picture. **Read** the sentences.
- **Circle** the correct possessive pronoun in parentheses.

1. Mr. Sims is (our, ours) neighbor.

2. (His, Her) bird flew out of (it's, its) cage.

3. Did you find a yellow bird in (yours, your) tree?

4. That bird is (his, theirs).

Assess

- **Write** a sentence about the yellow bird. Use the possessive pronoun *its*.

_____

Pronouns and Antecedents

Practice

- **Look** at the picture. **Read** the sentences.
- **Circle** the correct pronoun in each sentence. The antecedent is underlined for you.

1. Cecilia wanted to surprise <u>Ali</u> on (her, their) birthday.

2. Cecilia bought <u>balloons</u> and gave (they, them) to Ali.

3. <u>Ali</u> said, "(I, We) am so surprised!"

4. <u>Balloons</u> are fun, and (them, they) make people happy.

Assess

- **Look** at the picture again. **Write** another sentence about the balloons. Use the word *they* or *them.*

Indefinite and Reflexive Pronouns

Practice

- **Look** at the picture. **Read** the sentences.
- **Circle** the correct pronoun in parentheses to complete each sentence.

1. (Other, Someone) left a note on my desk.

2. I read it out loud to (myself, itself).

3. It said that (everyone, either) thinks I am a good writer.

4. (Somethings, No one) heard me read the note.

5. Maybe the writer of the note will identify (himself, ourselves).

Assess

- **Write** a sentence about yourself. Use a reflexive pronoun.

Articles, Adjectives, and Adverbs

Transition to English

Articles
- Spanish speakers may use the word *one* in place of the article *a* (or *an*), just as *un/una* is used in Spanish. Students may use *ones* as a plural article.
- English learners may use (or omit) the article *the* differently from native English speakers—*I like the science; my cousin is nurse.*

Grammar *in Action*

Articles in a News Article
Copy and distribute a simple newspaper article. Read it aloud and have students follow along, highlighting the articles they encounter.

Articles

Introduce Say: *I need a pencil.* Hold up a pencil and say: *Here is a pencil with an eraser. The pencil is yellow.* Show some pencils: *The pencils are new.* Explain that *a*, *an*, and *the* are called *articles*: Articles are these words that come before nouns: *A pencil, the paper, an ink pen.* Use *a* or *an* before a singular noun. You can use *the* before singular nouns or plural nouns.

Teach Present the concept and provide examples:
- *A*, *an*, and *the* are articles.
- Use *a* before a singular noun that begins with a consonant sound; use *an* before a singular noun that begins with a vowel sound.

Articles
I want <u>a</u> banana. Sue wants <u>an</u> apple.
<u>The</u> fruit salad was good. <u>The</u> girls ate it all.

Practice/Assess Copy and distribute page 117. Explain that *an* is used before a word beginning with silent *h*. (See answers on page 129.)

Transition to English

Adjectives
- Spanish adjectives have endings that match the gender and number of nouns they modify. Assure students that English adjectives do not have these endings.
- In Spanish and Vietnamese, adjectives often follow nouns.

Grammar *in Action*

Who Am I? Have a student describe a classmate: *She is smart. She is quiet. She is wearing a blue sweater.* Whoever guesses correctly gives the next clues.

Adjectives

Size, What Kind, How Many

Introduce Say: *You know that nouns are words that name people, places, animals, or things—for example, girls and house. Adjectives are words that tell more about the nouns: small house, four girls, blue car, long hair. Which words are the adjectives?* (small, four, blue, long)

Teach Present the concept and provide examples:
- An adjective tells more about a noun or pronoun.

	Adjectives
What Kind?	a <u>good</u> friend; The food is <u>spicy.</u>
How Many?	<u>two</u> men; <u>many</u> apples
Size	a <u>big</u> hat; The school was <u>small.</u>

Practice/Assess Copy and distribute page 118. Explain the chart to students. (See answers on page 129.)

© Pearson Education, Inc.

Comparative and Superlative Adjectives

Introduce Draw three long lines of different lengths on the board. Point to the different lines and say: *This line is long. This line is longer. This line is the longest.* Say: Long *is an adjective.* Longer *compares two nouns, like two lines. To compare two nouns, add* -er *to most adjectives.* Longest *compares three or more nouns. To make a superlative adjective, add* -est *to most adjectives.*

Teach Present the concept and provide examples:
- Many comparative adjectives end in *-er: faster, thinner, tinier.* Change the spelling of some adjectives, like *tiny,* when you add *-er.*
- Many longer adjectives use the word *more* instead of *-er: more exciting, more beautiful.*
- Many superlative adjectives end in *-est: brightest, loudest, tallest.* Use *most* with longer adjectives: *most beautiful.*
- Some adjectives have irregular forms, such as *good, better, best.*

Comparative	Superlative
bigger; more important	fastest; most difficult

Practice/Assess Copy and distribute page 119. Discuss the completed sentences. (See answers on page 129.)

Demonstrative Adjectives

Introduce Present three girls and three boys, with the boys farther away. Ask: *Which students are girls? These students are girls. Those students are boys. Which girl is Tina? This girl is Tina. That boy is Ben.* These, those, this, *and* that *are called demonstrative adjectives. They help you demonstrate, or show, which one or which ones. Use* this *and* these *when things are close. Use* that *and* those *when things are far.*

Teach Present the concept and provide examples:
- Demonstrative adjectives: *this, that, these, those*

	Demonstrative Adjectives
Singular	<u>This</u> book is longer than <u>that</u> book.
Plural	<u>These</u> shoes are bigger than <u>those</u> shoes.

Practice/Assess Copy and distribute page 120. Remind students that *this* and *that* are used with singular nouns. (See answers on page 129.)

Transition to English

Comparative and Superlative Adjectives
Speakers of African and Asian languages may use English adjectives in patterns from their first languages: *She was the most fastest runner. My story is less longer than yours.*

Grammar *in Action*

Classroom Comparisons
Have pairs of students find pairs or sets of objects in the classroom to compare. For example, one pencil might be longer than another, while one book might be the heaviest of three. Have pairs present their findings.

Transition to English

This and That
In certain languages, including Korean, the relationship between expressing *this* and *that* and *here* and *there* does not correspond exactly to the way these terms are used in English. Clarify that the words *this* and *that* can modify nouns.

Grammar *in Action*

Concentration Provide two sets of word cards for a game of Concentration. Place both sets face down, and have students find matching pairs. As they play, they should say: *I want this card, I want that card,* or *These cards match.*

Articles, Adjectives, and Adverbs

Adverbs

- English learners may use adjectives as adverbs. Help students use adverbs.
- Point out to Spanish speakers that the adverb suffix *-ly* is like the ending *-mente* in Spanish. Give examples with cognates such as *rapidly/rápidamente*.

Grammar *in Action*

Walk This Way Write adverbs on slips of paper: *slowly, quickly, loudly, sleepily.* Display them. Have a volunteer choose one. Give a command, such as *Walk to the door.* The volunteer must walk in the manner of the adverb. The student who guesses the adverb takes the next turn.

Adverbs

Adverbs for When, Where, and How

Introduce Say and act out this chant: *Slowly I turn. Loudly I clap! I walk here and there. I end with a tap.* Say: Slowly, loudly, here, and there *are adverbs. They tell how, when, or where something happens.*

Teach Present the concept and provide examples:
- Adverbs tell more about the actions of verbs.
- Adverbs that tell *how* something happens often end in *-ly.*

	Adverbs
When?	I <u>always</u> walk to school.
Where?	I like to walk <u>outside</u>.
How?	I walk <u>quickly</u>.

Practice/Assess Copy and distribute page 121. Explain that an adverb can come before or after the verb. (See answers on page 129.)

Comparative Adverbs
English phrases can be challenging for students whose home languages use different phrasing, and students may say or write: *running quickly more than you* or *studying more hard than you.* Model sentences with comparative adverbs.

Grammar *in Action*

Favorite Athletes Display 3 pictures of athletes. Have students compare them, using *well, better, best* or *fast, faster, fastest* with verbs *run, play,* or *swim.*

Comparative and Superlative Adverbs

Introduce Say each sentence: *I speak quietly. Katya speaks more quietly. Raúl speaks most quietly.* More quietly *is a comparative adverb. It compares two actions: I speak, Katya speaks.* Most quietly *is a superlative adverb. It compares three or more actions. If an adverb does not end in -ly, add -er or -est to compare.*

Teach Present the concept and provide examples:
- A comparative adverb compares two actions.
- A superlative adverb compares three or more actions.
- Some adverbs are irregular: *well, better, best*

Comparative and Superlative Adverbs
Julia runs <u>fast</u>. Anil sings <u>beautifully</u>.
Pat runs <u>faster</u>. Kenji sings <u>more beautifully</u>.
Tere runs the <u>fastest</u>. Ivan sings <u>most</u> beautifully.

Practice/Assess Copy and distribute page 122. Remind students that *more* or *most* are not added to an adverb that already has an *-er* or *-est* ending. (See answers on page 129.)

© Pearson Education, Inc.

Name _____

Articles

Practice

- **Look** at the picture. **Read** the sentences.
- **Circle** the article in parentheses that completes each sentence.

1. Cali, Beth, and Lyn found (an, a) rope in their garage.

2. (An, The) rope was six feet long.

3. Beth knew (a, an) song for jumping rope.

4. (The, A) girls jumped rope for (a, an) hour.

Assess

- What can you do for an hour? **Write** about it here. Use articles.

_____

Name _____

Adjectives for Size, What Kind, How Many

Practice

- **Look** at the picture. **Read** the story.
- **Circle** the adjectives in the story.

My two brothers and I have a small garden. We have three plants. The plants have many

tomatoes that are big and red. They are delicious!

Assess

- **Write** the adjectives from the story in the chart.

Size	What Kind	How Many

ELL and Transition Handbook

Name _____

Comparative and Superlative Adjectives

Practice

- **Look** at the picture. **Read** the sentences.
- **Write** the correct adjective to complete each sentence.

Hercules   Maxine   Chico

1. Hercules is _____ than Chico. (smaller, smallest)

2. Chico is the _____ of the three dogs. (largest, larger)

3. Maxine is _____ than Hercules. (more beautiful, beautifulest)

4. The big dog should have a _____ name. (gooder, better)

5. Hercules has the _____ name of all. (funniest, funnier)

Assess

- **Write** your own sentence that compares one of the dogs to another dog.

_____

Demonstrative Adjectives

Practice

- **Look** at the picture. **Read** the sentences.
- **Circle** the correct adjective to complete each sentence.

1. (These, This) flowers are called poppies.

2. Each spring, (this, these) field is full of poppies.

3. (That, Those) tree on the hill looks like a person.

4. People ride their bikes in (those, this) hills.

5. Many people take pictures of (this, these) place.

Assess

- **Look** at the picture again. **Write** another sentence about the field. Use *this, that, these,* or *those.*

Adverbs for When, Where, and How

Practice

- **Look** at the picture. **Read** the sentences.
- **Circle** the correct adverb for each sentence.

1. My sister sings (loudly, neatly).

2. I stand (outside, below) and listen.

3. She sings (beautifully, safely)!

4. I (always, yesterday) like listening to my sister sing.

Assess

- **Write** a sentence that tells how, when, or where you do something. Use an adverb.

_____

Comparative and Superlative Adverbs

Practice

- **Look** at the picture. **Read** the sentences.
- **Circle** the correct adverb to complete each sentence.

1. The stars shine (more brightly, brightly) in the country than in the city.

2. The dogs bark (louder, more louder) here.

3. I sleep (better, goodly) with the window closed.

4. People walk (more faster, faster) in the city.

5. This is the place I like to visit (later, most).

Assess

- Do you like the city or the country better? **Write** a sentence about it.
  Include an adverb.

© Pearson Education, Inc.

Prepositions and Prepositional Phrases

Introduce Stand behind a chair, and have students do the same. Say: *Behind the chair,* and have students repeat. Continue moving and speaking with *beside, around,* and *on* (sit). Explain: Behind, beside, around, *and* on *are prepositions.* Behind the chair *and* on it *are prepositional phrases.* Behind *is a preposition, and* chair *is a noun.* On *is a preposition, and* it *is a pronoun.*

Teach Present the concept and provide examples:
- A prepositional phrase can tell where, when, how, or which one.
- A prepositional phrase begins with a preposition (*above, across, at, behind, for, from, in, near, with,* and so on).
- It ends with a noun or pronoun.

Preposition	around
Prepositional Phrase	around the chair

Practice/Assess Copy and distribute page 124. Help students describe the picture. (See answers on page 129.)

© Pearson Education, Inc.

Conjunctions

Introduce Use colored pens or markers to illustrate: *I have a red pen <u>and</u> a green pen.* The word *and* joins two similar things: two colors of pens. *Do you like red <u>or</u> green better?* The word *or* gives a choice: red or green. *You can use the green pen, <u>but</u> don't use the red pen right now.* The word *but* joins two different ideas: use and don't use. *Or, but,* and *and are called* conjunctions.

Teach Present the concept and provide examples:
- A conjunction joins words, phrases, and sentences.

Related ideas: *Pak <u>and</u> I are friends.*
Different ideas: *We live far apart, <u>but</u> we talk often.*
Choice: *We talk on the phone <u>or</u> we send e-mail.*

Practice/Assess Copy and distribute page 125. Help students name the items in the picture. (See answers on page 129.)

Transition to English

Prepositional Phrases
Prepositional phrases will be familiar to speakers of various languges, but students may choose prepositions based on home-language usage or meanings: *in Friday; on April; until there.*

Grammar *in Action*

Following Directions
Model as you give students directions to follow: *Walk to this side of the room. Walk across the room. Stand by a desk. Look under the desk,* and so on. Have volunteers take turns giving directions that include prepositional phrases.

Transition to English

Conjunctions
Speakers of Chinese and some other languages may build sentences using two conjunctions where English typically uses one: *Because the sun came up, so I could see the clock.* Help students practice English patterns.

Grammar *in Action*

Common Phrases Share these common phrases with conjunctions: *salt and pepper; thanks, but no thanks; stop-and-go traffic; left or right; boy or girl.* Invite students to say them while using gestures to help show the meanings.

Prepositions

Practice

- **Look** at the picture. **Read** the sentences.
- **Circle** the correct preposition to complete each sentence.

1. We are (behind, at) the lake.

2. I play a game called "catch" (with, over) my dad.

3. Jeff walks (after, near) the water.

4. Mom sits (under, on) a chair and reads.

5. Ducks swim (in, from) the water.

Assess

- **Write** a sentence about the lake. Use a prepositional phrase.

Conjunctions

Practice

- **Look** at the picture. **Read** the sentences.
- **Circle** the correct conjunction to complete each sentence.

1. Are you ready to order, (but, or) do you want me to come back later?

2. I want a tuna sandwich, (and, or) the young lady wants a cheeseburger.

3. Do you want fries, (or, but) do you want a salad with your lunch?

4. I would like a salad, (or, but) please do not put salad dressing on it.

Assess

- What do you think the waiter said next? **Write** a sentence that has one of these words: *and, but, or.*

Answer Key

page 68: Common Nouns

Practice
People: father, boys, woman; **Places:** soccer field, playground, park office; **Animals:** rabbit, squirrel; **Things:** swing, ball, bike

Assess
Answers will vary. Students should write the names of items found in the classroom.

page 69: Special Names

Practice
Names of Children: Alex, Tuan, Karen;
Names of Animals: Spot, Lulu, Goldie, Speedy;
Names of Places: Greenview School, Hope Garden; Barton Library

Assess
Answers will vary. Students should write the names of specific places and people, beginning each name with a capital letter.

page 70: Titles and Abbreviations

Practice
1. Mr. Turner; **2.** Dr. Lisa Johnson;
3. Miss Eva Santos; **4.** Mr. Mark Tanaka

Assess
Answers will vary. Verify that students include a title such as Mr., Ms., and Dr. when writing each name of adults they know.

page 71: Days, Months, and Holidays

Practice
1. Thanksgiving; **2.** Veterans Day; **3.** Friday, November 30; **4.** Tuesday, November 6;
5. on Wednesdays

Assess
1. Sunday, Monday, Tuesday, Wednesday, Thursday, Friday, Saturday; **2.** Answers will vary. Students should begin the name of each holiday and each month with a capital letter.

page 72: Singular and Plural Nouns

Practice
Singular Nouns: nest, bird, sun;
Plural Nouns: men, butterflies, feet, leaves, benches

Assess
Answers will vary but should include three singular and three plural nouns. Students should write the names of items found in the classroom.

page 73:
Singular and Plural Possessive Nouns

Practice
1. Today's; **2.** children's; **3.** reader's; **4.** ladies'

Assess
Answers will vary. For sentences using singular possessive nouns, students may choose *reader's* or *today's*. For sentences using plural possessive nouns, students may choose *children's* or *ladies'*.

page 79: Verbs in Present Tense

Practice
1. wait; **2.** talks; **3.** sits; **4.** see

Assess
Answers will vary, but students may write a sentence such as *The dog barks.*

page 80:
Verbs in Past Tense

Practice
1. celebrated; **2.** gave; **3.** played; **4.** made;
5. had

Assess
Answers will vary, but students may write *We ate cake and ice cream.*

page 81: Verbs in Future Tense

Practice
The mother bird <u>will find</u> food for the babies. In a few days, she <u>will teach</u> them to fly. Soon, the baby birds <u>will grow</u> big and strong. They <u>will fly</u> away from the nest.

Assess
Answers will vary, but students may write a sentence such as *The mother bird will go too.*

page 82:
Principal Parts of Regular Verbs

Practice
1. *has started*, past participle; **2.** *listen*, present;
3. *are playing*, present participle; **4.** *has played*, past participle; **5.** *plays*, present

Assess
Answers will vary, but students may write a sentence such as *Ray is playing the flute.*

page 83: Principal Parts of Irregular Verbs

Practice

1. *went*, past; **2.** *go*, present; **3.** *have grown*, past participle; **4.** *am growing*, present participle

Assess

Answers will vary, but students may write a sentence such as *The doctor wrote on the chart.*

page 84: Helping Verbs

Practice

1. are learning; **2.** have seen; **3.** am using; **4.** will give

Assess

Answers will vary, but students may write a sentence such as *She will tell her friends about dolphins.*

page 85: Linking Verbs

Practice

1. *am*; **2.** *feel*; **3.** *seems*; **4.** *is*

Assess

Answers will vary, but students may write *The girl is sick.*

page 86: Contractions and Negatives

Practice

1. *I'm*; **2.** *Shouldn't*; **3.** *I've*; **4.** *You're*; **5.** *ever*

Assess

Answers will vary, but students may write *The dad didn't know she already did her homework.*

page 94: Subjects and Predicates

Practice

1. The farmer's market / is a busy place;
2. The sun / shines brightly today;
3. A man / sells big, red tomatoes;
4. A woman / puts carrots into her bag.

Assess

Answers will vary, but students may begin the sentence with "*A woman.*"

page 95: Subject-Verb Agreement

Practice

1. gives; **2.** enjoy; **3.** throw; **4.** likes

Assess

Answers will vary. Check for subject-verb agreement.

page 96: Word Order

Practice

1. We went to the zoo; **2.** I saw the elephants; **3.** The giraffes were tall.

Assess

Answers will vary, but make sure students start sentences with the subject or use another word order that makes sense.

page 97: Complete Sentences and Sentence Fragments

Practice

1. The baker bakes bread. **2.** He puts the bread into the oven. **3.** He makes delicious pies.

Assess

Answers will vary but should be complete sentences.

page 98: Statements and Questions

Practice

1. This is Raquel's party. **2.** Do you like to dance? **3.** Raquel's mom takes pictures. **4.** Len eats pizza. **5.** What time is it?

Assess

Answers will vary; possible questions: *Did you go to Raquel's party? Was it fun? When did the party begin?*

page 99: Exclamations and Interjections

Practice

Runner would think: "I am running fast!"
Friend would say: "Hooray! You will win!"
Crying boy would say: "I want to go home!"

Assess

Answers will vary. Encourage students to imagine themselves winning at a school or sports competition. Some suggestions: *Hooray! Wow! I worked so hard!*

page 100: Commands

Practice

Sentences 2 and 3 are commands.

Assess

Answers will vary, but students may write *First, find a pitcher and some lemons. Cut the lemons. Squeeze the lemons. Add water, sugar, and ice.*

page 101: Simple and Compound Sentences

Practice

1. Mom needs to go to work. Jon is still eating his cereal. **2.** Jon needs to hurry. Mom will be late for work. **3.** Jon finishes his cereal. They both run out the door.

Assess

Answers will vary, but students may write *Jon will not be late for school, and Mom will not be late for work.*

page 102: Combining Sentences

Practice

1. Dad and I went to the park. **2.** Dad sat on a bench and read his book. **3.** I found a stick and threw it. **4.** My dog ran far and got the stick.

Assess

Answers will vary, but sample answers include: *My friend and I went to the park; Dad drove us there and read his book. I played with my friend and with my dog. My dog was happy and playful.*

page 103: Complex Sentences

Practice

These sentences are complex: **1.** I watch Tran because she is a good painter; **2.** Since this painting is big, Tran will put it in Mom's room; **3.** She will start it when she finishes this one.

Assess

Answers will vary, but students may write sentences such as *When Tran finishes this painting, she will make another one. Since Tran's sister wants a painting, Tran will make one.*

page 104: Independent and Dependent Clauses

Practice

1. After I do my homework; **2.** When David is there; **3.** until we are very tired; **4.** because he has homework.

Assess

Answers will vary, but sample answers include: *When David goes home, I go home also* or *When David goes home, he does his homework.*

page 105: Commas

Practice

1. Gino's, the new Italian restaurant, has great food; **2.** Mom, thank you for buying us dinner; **3.** I want soup, salad, pizza, and lemonade; **4.** Well, I hope you can eat all that!

Assess

Answers will vary, but make sure students use a comma after each menu item in the series.

page 109: Subject Pronouns

Practice

1. I; **2.** We; **3.** They; **4.** she

Assess

Answers will vary, but students may write a sentence such as *They were late for school.*

page 110: Object Pronouns

Practice

1. me; **2.** us; **3.** them; **4.** them

Assess

Answers will vary, but students may write a sentence such as *Jen gave the cookies to him.*

page 111: Possessive Pronouns

Practice

1. our; **2.** His, its; **3.** your; **4.** his

Assess

Answers will vary, but students may write a sentence such as *The bird will fly to its cage.*

page 112: Pronouns and Antecedents

Practice
1. her; **2.** them; **3.** I; **4.** they

Assess
Answers will vary, but students may write a sentence such as *Ali loved the balloons because they were from her friend.*

page 113: Indefinite and Reflexive Pronouns

Practice
1. Someone; **2.** myself; **3.** everyone; **4.** No one; **5.** himself

Assess
Answers will vary, but students may write a sentence such as *I like to teach myself English words.*

page 117: Articles

Practice
1. a; **2.** The; **3.** a; **4.** The, an

Assess
Answers will vary, but students may write a sentence such as *I can play baseball for an hour.*

page 118: Adjectives for Size, What Kind, How Many

Practice
two; small; three; many; big; red; delicious

Assess
Size: small, big; **What Kind:** red, delicious; **How Many:** two, three, many

page 119: Comparative and Superlative Adjectives

Practice
1. smaller; **2.** largest; **3.** more beautiful; **4.** better; **5.** funniest

Assess
Answers will vary, but students may write a sentence such as *Maxine is larger than Hercules.*

page 120: Demonstrative Adjectives

Practice
1. These; **2.** this; **3.** That; **4.** those; **5.** this

Assess
Answers will vary, but students may write a sentence such as *This field is beautiful.*

page 121: Adverbs for When, Where, and How

Practice
1. loudly; **2.** outside; **3.** beautifully; **4.** always

Assess
Answers will vary, but students may write a sentence such as *I run quickly.*

page 122: Comparative and Superlative Adverbs

Practice
1. more brightly; **2.** louder; **3.** better; **4.** faster; **5.** most

Assess
Answers will vary, but students may write a sentence such as *I like the city better.*

page 124: Prepositions

Practice
1. at; **2.** with; **3.** near; **4.** on; **5.** in

Assess
Answers will vary, but students may write a sentence such as *Ducks live near the lake.*

page 125: Conjunctions

Practice
1. or; **2.** and; **3.** or; **4.** but

Assess
Answers will vary, but students may write a sentence such as *Thank you for your order, and I will be back soon.*

Part 3
Phonics Instruction for English Language Learners

Contents

Introduction to the Phonics Transition Lessons

Phonemic awareness, phonics, and word study are critical components of literacy instruction for English language learners. The core lessons in *Scott Foresman Reading Street* provide the explicit, systematic instruction that all students need to become fluent readers and writers. The following Phonics Transition Lessons and reproducible Practice Pages will supplement the core instruction with customized lessons that meet the particular needs of English language learners. Lessons and Practice Pages are divided into three sections:

- **Concepts of Print** English language learners may be unfamiliar with English print conventions, such as the English alphabet, word and sentence boundaries, and left-to-right directionality. This section provides activities that can be used at any time to develop students' understanding of concepts of print.

- **Problem Sounds in English** These lessons cover the phonemes that are typically the most challenging for English language learners, such as easily confused consonants and short vowel sounds. In some cases, a Model Lesson is provided along with notes for using the same lesson format to teach related phonics skills. Lessons in this section include Pronunciation Tips that teachers can use to help students produce the target phonemes. A Practice Page for every lesson provides strong visual support for instruction and offers additional practice.

- **Word Study** An understanding of word parts and word origins is a powerful tool for English language learners. The Word Study Lessons reinforce the core instruction and include suggestions for making connections with the home language. The Practice Pages provide visual support and context for the target skills.

Throughout the Phonics Transition Lessons, a **Transition to English** feature identifies specific challenges faced by English language learners when acquiring the target skills.

In addition to the Phonics Transition Lessons and Practice Pages, you can supplement core phonics instruction with routines such as the following:

- **Build phonological and phonemic awareness.** If students have not learned to distinguish word boundaries, syllables, rhymes, or phonemes within words, carry out activities such as having students count the words in a sentence or the syllables in a word; having students identify rhyming and non-rhyming words; and having students segment and blend the syllables or phonemes within a word.

- **Strengthen oral language skills.** Allow beginning speakers to work with partners when completing phonics activities. Encourage students to talk about their work with English, and provide other oral language opportunities with the target words.

- **Teach word meanings.** Before teaching the phonics skills, introduce the target words orally to students by using them in activities such as chants and riddle games, or asking and answering questions that use the words.

- **Provide alternate instruction.** If students have limited literacy skills, use the Scott Foresman Reading Intervention program to provide literacy instruction at the level where children can participate and learn.

- **Relate to the home language.** Whenever possible, help students build on what they already know by making connections between the target phonics skill and the home language. Use available resources, such as bilingual staff members, bilingual dictionaries, language Web sites, and the students themselves, to gather information about the home language.

- **Engage students as active learners.** Students who are acquiring English may have a stronger awareness of language than monolingual speakers. Build their knowledge with engaging activities that explicitly show the patterns and structures of language. Consider games such as the following:

Four by Four

Use with page 134.

Make and distribute copies of page 134. Work with students to generate a class list of twenty or more words that reflect the target phonics or word study skills that students have recently studied—for example, words that begin with the prefixes *im-* and *in-*. Write each word on a card. Have students choose sixteen words from the list and write them in random order in the squares on page 134. Have students cut out the star markers at the bottom of the page. Shuffle the cards, and read aloud one card at a time. Students should look for each word on their paper and cover it with a star marker. The first one to have four marked words in a row (horizontally, vertically, or diagonally) calls out "Four by Four!" Note: For students in early stages of literacy, write consonants in the squares, and have students listen for words that begin with the consonants.

Word Hunt

Use with page 135.

Choose a target phonics or word study skill, such as "Words with long *a*" or "Words with the suffix *-ly*," and list it at the top of page 135. Make and distribute copies to individuals, partners, or small groups. Have students look around the classroom and school, in books and magazines, and perhaps at home, for words that have the particular phonics feature. They can list the words in the chart on page 135, and either draw or attach (with glue or tape) pictures that illustrate the words. Conclude by having students share the words they find.

Four by Four

- **Write** the words that your teacher gives you. Write one word in each square.
- **Listen** to the words. When you hear a word that is in a square, **cover** it with a star marker.
- When you have four covered words in a row, **say** "Four by Four!"

- **Cut out** the star markers. **Use** them in the game.

Name _____

Word Hunt: Words with _____

- **Find** words that share a sound or a spelling pattern.
- **Write** the words. **Add** pictures or definitions for the words.
- **Tell** your words to a friend.

Word	Picture or Definition

Print Awareness

Transition to English

Many factors can influence students' understanding of print conventions. The students may be emergent readers of non-alphabetic languages or languages with alphabets similar to or different from the English alphabet. Some English learners may be familiar with reading left to right and top to bottom, as in English. Others may be accustomed to reading text from right to left, or from the bottom to the top of the page. Some have little experience with printed text. For students who are unfamiliar with English print conventions, activities such as these will help develop print awareness and strengthen literacy skills.

Print Awareness Activities

Parts of a Book Show students how to hold a book. Point out and explain the title, author byline, and illustrator's name. Turn to the selection pages and read a sentence or two. Discuss how the illustrations go with the text. Page through the book, and show how the narrative continues. Point to the text on each page. Then have students practice holding the book correctly, finding the title and author's name, turning the pages, and pointing to the text on each page.

Words, Sentences, Paragraphs Display a few paragraphs of printed text in a large format or on an overhead transparency. Frame one word with your fingers, and read it aloud. Explain that it is a word, and point out the spacing before and after the word. Then read aloud a sentence, running your finger under each word as you read. Point out the sentence boundaries: a capital letter at the beginning of the sentence and the end punctuation. Then circle a paragraph with your finger, and explain that a paragraph is a group of related sentences. Point out the indent at the beginning of the paragraph. Have students practice finding words, sentences, and paragraphs in other texts.

Directionality As you read a book aloud, put your finger on the starting point in the text on each page. Show that you read from left to right and from top to bottom by moving your finger along lines of text. Use your finger to show how to sweep back from the end of a line to the beginning of another, and how to move to the next page. Then have students use their fingers to show the correct movement as you read the text aloud again.

Writing the Alphabet Students should be introduced systematically to all the letters of the English alphabet, in manuscript and cursive writing. Students can practice writing letters, punctuation marks, and numbers, using pages 137, 138, and 139 as handwriting guides.

Name _____

The Alphabet

- **Practice** writing the letters of the alphabet.
- **Write** more of the letters on other paper.

Name _____

The D'Nealian™ Alphabet

- **Practice** writing the letters of the alphabet.
- **Write** more of the letters on other paper.

a b c d e f g h i j k

l m n o p q r s t

u v w x y z

A B C D E F G H I J K

L M N O P Q R S T

U V W X Y Z

1 2 3 4 5 6 7 8 9 10

The D'Nealian™ Cursive Alphabet

- **Practice** writing the letters of the alphabet in cursive.
- **Write** more of the letters on other paper.

a b c d e f g h i j k

l m n o p q r s t

u v w x y z

A B C D E F G H I J K

L M N O P Q R S T

U V W X Y Z

1 2 3 4 5 6 7 8 9 10

Confusing Consonants

Transition to English

The phonemes of certain English consonants may be unfamiliar to English language learners or easily confused with other phonemes. For example, consonant digraphs such as /th/, /sh/, and /ch/ may sound alike to some English language learners. Spanish speakers may hear and write /n/ at the end of words ending with /m/. The following lessons provide practice with certain consonant pairs that English language learners may find troublesome. You can develop similar lessons for other consonant sounds that are difficult for your students. This model lesson gives you a pattern for teaching.

☆ Model Lesson: Words with *b* and *v*　　　Use with page 143.

Introduce Copy and distribute page 143. Have students point to the picture of the box at the top of the page. Say: *This is a box. The word* box *begins with /b/. Say it with me: /b/, /b/, /b/, box.* Repeat the procedure with the word *van*, using the other picture at the top of the page.

Teach Guide students to distinguish between /b/ and /v/, using the Pronunciation Tip. Then, direct students' attention to Row 1. Name each of the items shown, one by one: *boat, vest, bat, vase.* Continue: *I'll say each word one more time. If the word starts with the letter* b, *circle* b *under the picture. If the word starts with the letter* v, *circle* v. Read the words aloud once more, giving students enough time to circle the corresponding letter.
　Repeat the process for Row 2, omitting the directions: *violin, vine, basketball, bike.*

Practice Have students look at the pictures in Row 3. Ask them to tell what the pictures show *(box, van)* and then write those words on the appropriate blank line.
　Read the practice sentence aloud and have students find the words with *b* and *v (Val, Billy, dove, wave).* After they've had a chance to repeat the sentence several times, challenge students to say it as quickly as they can.

Assess Make letter cards for *b* and *v*, and give one of each to each student. Tell students: *I will say some words. Hold up the card that matches the sound you hear in each word:* boat, vote, bolt, volt, vanilla, basket, very, berry, bent, vent, best, vest, vane. Then have students repeat the contrasting word pairs after you, striving for the correct pronunciation of /b/ and /v/. Keep in mind that students who have difficulty distinguishing /b/ and /v/ may still be able to comprehend words they hear or read that start with these consonants.

> **Pronunciation Tip**
> *b* **and** *v When you say /b/, your lips start out together. Then they open and a tiny puff of air comes out of your mouth. If you touch your throat, you can feel it move because your voice box is on. Can you hold a /b/ sound? Try it: /b/, /b/. No, you can't hold it. When you say /v/, you can hold it: /vvvv/. Your voice box is still on. Your top teeth touch your bottom lip. Say /v/ and feel your teeth touch your bottom lip. Hold the sound. Try it: /vvvv/, /vvvv/. Try both sounds: /b/, /vvvv/.*

Adapting the ☆ **Model Lesson**

Use the same lesson format above to teach the following consonants and digraphs: /ch/, /sh/, /d/, /th/, /l/, /r/, /m/, /n/, and /s/. The following information will help you to customize each lesson.

Notes for Additional Lessons

Words with *ch* and *sh*

Use with page 144.

Teach Use these words: *child, shop.* Row 1 of page 144: *shoe, cherry, chair, sheep.*

Practice Row 2: *shark, shell, chicken, chalk.*
Row 3: *child, shop.* Practice sentence: *Sherry the Shark chewed and chewed on a shiny shoe.*

Assess Use these words: *chew, shoe, chin, shin, chomp, cherry, Sherry, shell, chain, chair, share.*

> **Pronunciation Tip**
> *ch* **and** *sh* *When you say /ch/, your lips are open and your teeth are close together. Your tongue moves as you make the sound. Can you hold a /ch/ sound? Try it: /ch/, /ch/. No, you can't hold it. When you say /sh/, your lips are also open and your teeth are close together. But your tongue doesn't move, and you can't hold the sound: /shhhhh/. Try it: /shhhhh/, /shhhhh/. Try both sounds: /ch/, /shhhhh/.*

Words with *d* and *th*

Use with page 145.

Teach Use these words: *desk, third.* Row 1 of page 145: *door, thorn, thirty, dinosaur.*

Practice Row 2: *thermos, thumb, dish, dog.*
Row 3: *third, desk.* Practice sentence: *Think a thought about a daring dog walking through thick grass.*

Assess Use these words: *thigh, dye, think, thirty, dirty, duck, though, dough, there, dare.*

> **Pronunciation Tip**
> *d* **and** *th* *When you say /d/, the tip of your tongue touches above your tip teeth. Say /d/ and feel the tip of your tongue touch above your top teeth: /d/. Is your voice box on? Yes, you can feel your throat move when you say /d/. Can you hold a /d/ sound? Try it: /d/, /d/. No, you can't hold it. When you say /TH/ in a word like this, your voice box is also on: /TH/. But your tongue is between your teeth, and you can hold the sound. Try it: /THHHHH/, /THHHHH/. Try both sounds: /d/, /THHHHH/. When you say /th/ in a word like thin, your voice box is off, and you can hold the sound: /thhhhh/. The tip of your tongue comes out between your teeth and air comes out, but no sound. Try it: /thhhhh/, /thhhhh/. Try both th sounds: /THHHHH/, /thhhhh/.*

Notes for Additional Lessons

Words with *l* and *r*
Use with page 146.

Teach Use these words: *leg, ring*. Row 1 of page 146: *radio, lake, light, ruler*.

Practice Row 2: *rose, lizard, leaf, river*.
Row 3: *leg, ring*. Practice sentence: *The red river runs into a little lake.*

Assess Use these words: *rake, lake, rip, lip, red, rice, late, rate, load, road, loud, lean.*

> **Pronunciation Tip**
> *l* **and** *r* When you say /l/, the tip of your tongue touches above your top teeth and stays there. Say /l/ and feel your throat move. Your voice box is on when you say /l/. Try it: /l/, /l/. When you say /r/, your voice box is on again. The tip of your tongue goes toward the roof of your mouth, but doesn't touch it. Try it: /r/, /r/. Try both sounds: /l/, /r/.

Words with *m* and *n*
Use with page 147.

Teach Use these words: *mask, nest*. Row 1 of page 147: *nose, net, mouse, match*.

Practice Focus on ending sounds for Row 2: *jam, pen, stem, fan*.
Row 3: *mask, nest*. Practice sentence: *The man in the moon eats ice cream with a spoon.*

Assess Use these words: *meat, neat, mole, next, moat, note, Pam, pan, tone, time, some, sun.*

> **Pronunciation Tip**
> *m* **and** *n* When you say /m/, your lips come together and a little air comes out of your nose. Can you hold the sound /m/? Try it: /mmmm/, /mmmm/. Yes, you can hold the sound. You can also hold the /n/ sound. Try it: /nnnn/. But when you say /n/, your lips are open. Your tongue is behind your top teeth. Say it again: /n/, /n/. Try both sounds: /m/, /n/.

Words with *s* and *th*
Use with page 148.

Teach Use these words: *sun, thorn*. Row 1 of page 148: *saw, thumb, thermos, soap*.

Practice Row 2: *sandwich, soup, thigh, thirteen*.
Row 3: *sun, thorn*. Practice sentence: *Sara sipped thick soup.*

Assess Use these words: *some, thumb, so, think, sink, sock, thin, thing, sing, thank.*

> **Pronunciation Tip**
> *s* **and** *th* When you say /s/, the tip of your tongue touches above your top teeth. It makes a snake sound, and you can hold the sound. Try it: /ssss/, /ssss/. When you say /th/ in a word like thick, the tip of your tongue comes out between your teeth. You can feel air come out of your mouth. Try it: /thhhh/, /thhhh/. Try both sounds: /ssss/, /thhhh/.

Name _____

Words with *b* and *v*

- If the word begins with the sound of *b* in *box*, **circle** the *b*.
- If the word begins with the sound of *v* in *van*, **circle** the *v*.

ROW 1

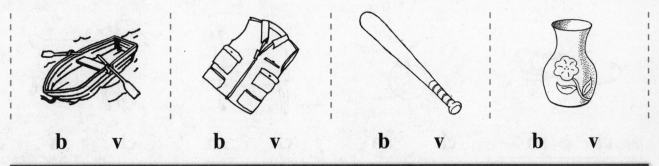

| b   v | b   v | b   v | b   v |

ROW 2

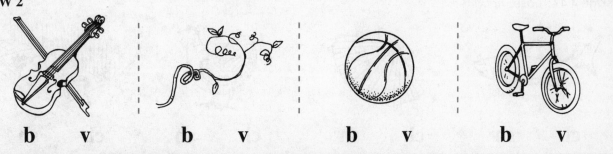

| b   v | b   v | b   v | b   v |

- **Look** at each picture. **Say** its name. **Write** the word.

ROW 3

_____   _____

Find *b* and *v* in this sentence. Then **practice** chanting or singing the sentence.

Val and Billy dove into the wave.

Name _____

Words with *ch* and *sh*

- If the word begins with the sound of *ch* in *child*, **circle** the *ch*.
- If the word begins with the sound of *sh* in *shop*, **circle** the *sh*.

ROW 1

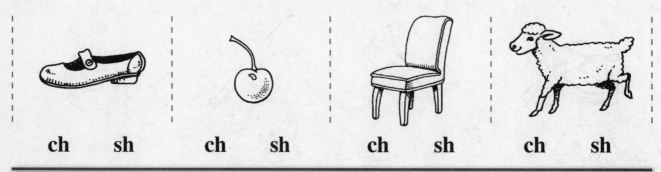

ch   sh   ch   sh   ch   sh   ch   sh

ROW 2

ch   sh   ch   sh   ch   sh   ch   sh

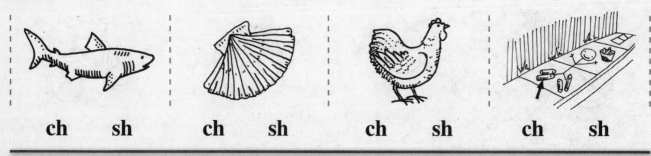

- **Look** at each picture. **Say** its name. **Write** the word.

ROW 3

_____   _____

Find *ch* and *sh* in this sentence. Then **practice** chanting or singing the sentence.

Sherry the Shark chewed and chewed on a shiny shoe.

Name _____

Words with *d* and *th*

- If the word begins with the sound of *d* in *desk*, **circle** the *d*.
- If the word begins with the sound of *th* in *third*, **circle** the *th*.

ROW 1

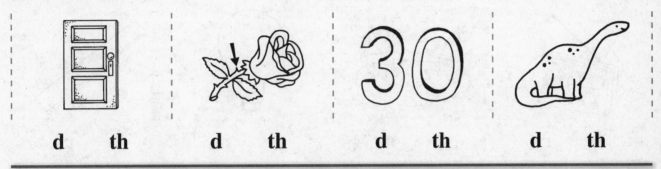

| d | th | d | th | d | th | d | th |

ROW 2

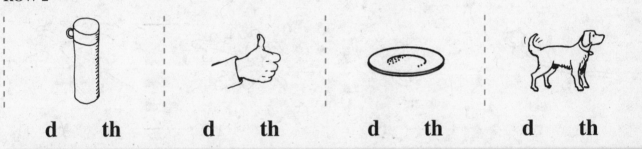

| d | th | d | th | d | th | d | th |

- **Look** at each picture. **Say** its name. **Write** the word.

ROW 3

_____   _____

Find *th* and *d* in this sentence. Then **practice** chanting or singing the sentence.

Think a thought about a daring dog walking through thick grass.

Name _____

Words with *l* and *r*

- If the word begins with the sound of *l* in *leg*, **circle** the *l*.
- If the word begins with the sound of *r* in *ring*, **circle** the *r*.

ROW 1

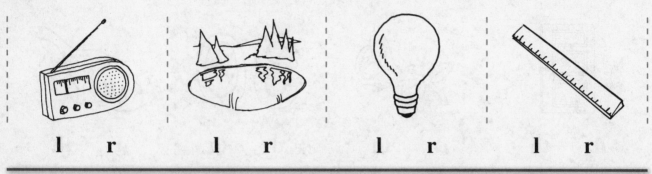

l   r   l   r   l   r   l   r

ROW 2

l   r   l   r   l   r   l   r

- **Look** at each picture. **Say** its name. **Write** the word.

ROW 3

_____   _____

Find *l* and *r* in this sentence. Then **practice** chanting or singing the sentence.

The red river runs into a little lake.

Words with *m* and *n*

- If the word has the sound of *m* in *mask*, **circle** the *m*.
- If the word has the sound of *n* in *nest*, **circle** the *n*.

ROW 1

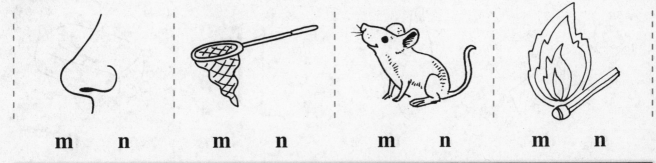

| m   n | m   n | m   n | m   n |

ROW 2

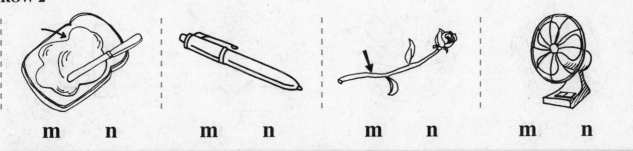

| m   n | m   n | m   n | m   n |

- **Look** at each picture. **Say** its name. **Write** the word.

ROW 3

_____   _____

Find *m* and *n* in this sentence. Then **practice** chanting or singing the sentence.

The man in the moon eats ice cream with a spoon.

Name _____

Words with *s* and *th*

- If the word begins with the sound of *s* in *sun*, **circle** the *s*.
- If the word begins with the sound of *th* in *thorn*, **circle** the *th*.

ROW 1

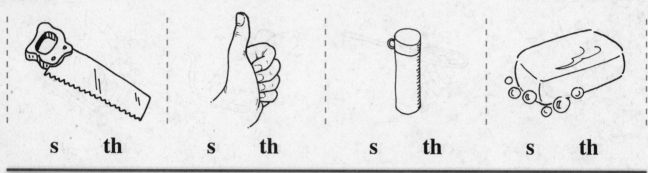

| s   th | s   th | s   th | s   th |

ROW 2

| s   th | s   th | s   th | s   th |

- **Look** at each picture. **Say** its name. **Write** the word.

ROW 3

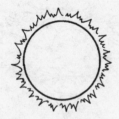   

_____   _____

Find *s* and *th* in this sentence. Then **practice** chanting or singing the sentence.

Sara sipped thick soup.

Transition to English

Consonant blends in English words often are challenging for English language learners because their home languages may not combine consonant phonemes in similar ways at the beginnings and ends of words. For example, consonant blends with *l* and *r* can be particularly difficult for speakers of Asian languages such as Chinese, Korean, and Vietnamese. Speakers of Arabic may insert vowel sounds between the consonants within a blend. The following lessons provide practice with consonant blends. If your students are struggling with particular blends, you can develop similar lessons targeted to those blends.

Initial Consonant Blends   Use with page 151.

Introduce Copy and distribute page 151. Have students point to the picture of the crib at the top of the page. Say: *This is a crib. The word* crib *begins with /cr/.* Write *crib* on the board. Say: *Usually, when two letters come before a vowel* (underline the *cr*), *we blend the sounds of the letters: /c/-/r/...,c/-/r/-/i/-/b/.* Say *it with me: /c/-/r/-/i/-/b/,* crib. Repeat for *clap.*

Teach Direct students' attention to Row 1. Name each of the items shown, one by one: *(crab, crown, clock, cloth).* Continue: *I'll say each word one more time. If the word starts with the letters* cr, *circle* cr *under the picture. If the word starts with the letters* cl, *circle* cl. Read the words aloud once more, giving students enough time to circle the corresponding letter.

Tell students that there are many beginning blends in English. Write a 10-column chart on the board with the headings *br, cr, cl, fl, gr, pr, pl, sn, sp, st.* List the words *crib* and *clap* in the columns where they belong. Add the words from Row 1 to the chart. Give several more examples. Invite children to suggest other words that begin with these blends that can be added to the chart.

Practice Have students look at the pictures in Row 2. Name the items shown *(princess, plant, price, plug),* and pause to let students circle their answer choices. Repeat the procedure for Row 3 *(straw, string, steak, starfish).*

Read the practice sentence aloud, and have students find the words with beginning blends *(clock, struck, students, snapped).* After they've had a chance to repeat the sentence several times, challenge students to say it as quickly as they can.

Assess Prepare sets of cards with a blend written on each one: *cr, cl, pr, pl, tr, dr, st, str.* Give each student a set of cards. Say a list of words, and have students display the correct initial blends: *crawl, please, claw, preen, tree, street, draw, stall.* Then have students repeat the words after you, striving for the correct pronunciation of the initial blends. Keep in mind that students who have difficulty pronouncing the initial blends may still be able to comprehend words they hear or read that start with these consonants.

**Pronunciation Tip
Initial Consonant
Blends** *When a word begins with two consonants like* c *and* r, *you blend the sounds of the two consonants together. In the word* crib, *take the /k/ sound and /r/ sound and put them together: /kr/. Try it: /kr/, /kr/, crib.*

Final Consonant Blends   Use with page 152.

Introduce Copy and distribute page 152. Have students point to the picture of the pond at the top of the page. Say: *This is a pond. The word* pond *ends with /nd/. Usually, when two letters come after a vowel* (underline the *nd*), *we blend the sounds of the letters: /n/-/d/...../p/-/o/-/n/-/d/. Say it with me:* pond, */p/-/o/-/n/-/d/.* Repeat for *sink.*

Teach Direct students' attention to Row 1. Name each of the items shown, one by one: *(band, trunk, hand, bank).* Continue: *I'll say each word one more time. If the word ends with the letters* nd, *circle* nd *under the picture. If the word ends with the letters* nk, *circle* nk. Read the words aloud once more, giving students enough time to circle the corresponding letter.

Tell students that there are many ending blends in English. Write a 9-column chart on the board with the headings *lt, mp, nch, nd, nk, nt, sk, sp, st.* List the words *pond* and *sink* in the columns where they belong. Add the words from Row 1 to the chart. Give several more examples. Invite children to suggest other words that end with these blends that can be added to the chart.

Practice Have students look at the pictures in Row 2. Name the items shown *(ant, paint, branch, inch)*, and pause to let students circle their answer choices. Repeat the procedure for Row 3 *(desk, vest, cast, mask).*

Read the practice sentence aloud, and have students find the words with ending blends *(must, ask, band, paint, bench).* After they've had a chance to read the sentence several times, challenge students to say it from memory.

Assess Prepare sets of cards with a blend written on each one: *nd, nk, nt, nch, sk, st.* Give each student a set of cards. Say a list of words, and have students display the correct final blends: *sink, cinch, bank, band, inch, ink, dusk, dust, ant, and, paint, pond.* Then have students repeat the words after you, striving for the correct pronunciation of the final blends. Keep in mind that students who have difficulty pronouncing the final blends may still be able to comprehend words they hear or read that end with these consonants.

> **Pronunciation Tip**
> **Final Consonant Blends** *When a word ends with two consonants like* s *and* k, *you blend the sounds of the two consonants together. In the word* desk, *take the /s/ sound and /k/ sound and put them together: /sk/. Try it: /sk/, /sk/,* desk.

Name _____

Initial Consonant Blends

- If the word begins with the sound of *cr* in *crib*, **circle** the *cr*.
- If the word begins with the sound of *cl* in *clap*, **circle** the *cl*.

ROW 1

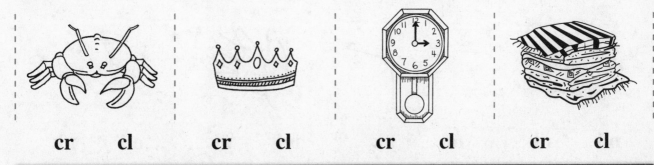

| cr cl | cr cl | cr cl | cr cl |

- If the word begins with the sound of *pl* in *plum*, **circle** the *pl*.
- If the word begins with the sound of *pr* in *prize*, **circle** the *pr*.

ROW 2

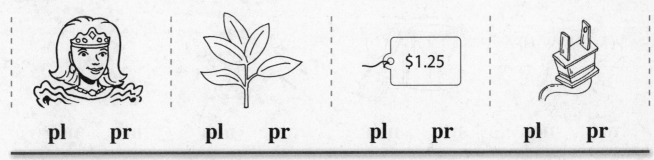

| pl pr | pl pr | pl pr | pl pr |

- If the word begins with the sound of *str* in *stripe*, **circle** the *str*.
- If the word begins with the sound of *st* in *stick*, **circle** the *st*.

ROW 3

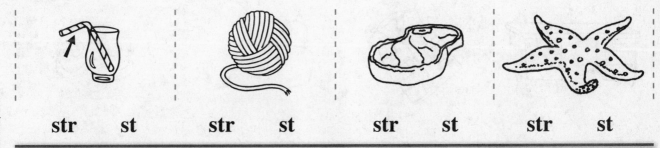

| str st | str st | str st | str st |

Find the beginning blends in this sentence. Then **practice** chanting or singing the sentence.

When the clock struck one, the students snapped their fingers.

Name _____

Final Consonant Blends

- If the word ends with the sound of *nd* in *pond*, **circle** the *nd*.
- If the word ends with the sound of *nk* in *sink*, **circle** the *nk*.

ROW 1

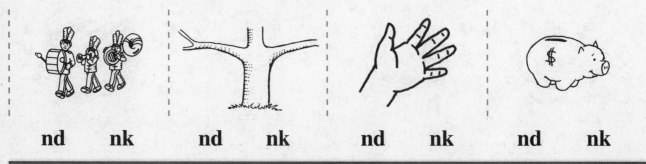

| nd nk | nd nk | nd nk | nd nk |

- If the word ends with the sound of *nt* in *cent*, **circle** the *nt*.
- If the word ends with the sound of *nch* in *bench*, **circle** the *nch*.

ROW 2

| nt nch | nt nch | nt nch | nt nch |

- If the word ends with the sound of *st* in *nest*, **circle** the *st*.
- If the word ends with the sound of *sk* in *tusk*, **circle** the *sk*.

ROW 3

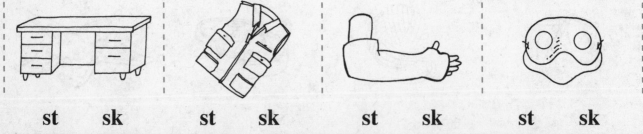

| st sk | st sk | st sk | st sk |

Find the ending blends in this sentence. Then **practice** chanting or singing the sentence.

You must ask the band to paint the bench.

Transition to English

Short vowel sounds may be challenging for many English language learners because in many languages, short vowel sounds may not exist or may only have approximations. For example, English language learners from various language backgrounds may pronounce short *i* like the *ee* in *see*. The following lessons provide practice for hearing and producing short vowel sounds. This model lesson gives you a pattern for teaching.

☆ Model Lesson: Short *a*   Use with page 155.

Introduce Copy and distribute page 155. Have students point to the apple at the top of the page. Say: *This is an apple. Apple begins with /a/. Say it with me: /a/, /a/, /a/, apple.*

Teach Tell students: *The /a/ sound is one sound of the letter a. We call this sound the short a. Repeat these /a/ words after me: cap, am, mat, pan.*

Ask students to name the items in Row 1 on page 155 *(acrobat, mop, bat, ant)*. Repeat each word, clearly pronouncing the vowel each time. Then say: *I'll say these words again. If you hear the /a/ sound, circle the picture:* acrobat, mop, bat, ant. Students should circle the *acrobat, bat,* and *ant* pictures—but not the *mop*.

Practice Have students look at the pictures in Row 2 on page 155. Have them read the words below each picture and circle the word that names it *(cap, man, map, can)*. Then have them look at the pictures in Row 3, say the name of each picture, and write the names *(man, bat, ant, hat)*.

Read the practice sentence aloud, and have students find the short *a* words *(acrobat, an, apple, bat, act)*. Invite students to chant the sentence together, clapping each time they hear short *a*.

Assess Tell students: *I will say some word pairs. Raise your hand when you hear the /a/ sound:* pat, pet; hot, hat; bad, bed; man, main; tug, tag. Then have students repeat the word pairs after you, striving for the correct pronunciation of /a/. Keep in mind that students who have difficulty pronouncing /a/ may still be able to comprehend short a words that they hear or read.

> **Pronunciation Tip**
> **short** *a When you say /a/, your jaw and tongue are down. Say /a/ and feel your jaw and tongue go down.*

Adapting the ☆ **Model Lesson**

Use the same lesson format above to teach the short vowels /e/, /i/, /o/, and /u/. The following information will help you to customize each lesson.

Short Vowels

Notes for Additional Lessons

Short e   Use with page 156.

Teach Use these /e/ words: *enter, exit, elephant, elk.* Row 1 of page 156: *vest, elephant, tiger, tent.*

Practice Row 2: *pen, web, bell, bed;* Row 3: *ten, bell, nest, web.* Practice sentence: *The elephant entered the tent with an elegant step.*

Assess Use these word pairs: *set, sat; ten, tan; net, not; sell, sale.*

> **Pronunciation Tip**
> **short e** When you say /e/, your mouth is open. Your tongue is behind your bottom teeth. Say /e/. Did your mouth open? Say /e/ again.

Short i   Use with page 157.

Teach Use these /i/ words: *it, sit, if, thin, with.* Row 1 of page 157: *dinner, gift, ice, inch.*

Practice Row 2: *pin, zip, dig, sit;* Row 3: *zip, gift, pig, six.* Practice sentence: *Six pigs with bibs grinned and did a jig in a minute.*

Assess Use these word pairs: *tin, ten; six, socks; pig, pine; trip, trap.*

> **Pronunciation Tip**
> **short i** When you say /i/, your mouth is open and your tongue is slightly lowered. Say /i/. Is your mouth open, and is your tongue slightly lowered? Practice: /i/. In Spanish, the letter *i* is pronounced /ē/. Point out that this letter has different sounds in English.

Short o   Use with page 158.

Teach Use these /o/ words: *on, olive, Oscar, opposite.* Row 1 of page 158: *elephant, dog, octopus, box.*

Practice Row 2: *lock, rock, fox, hop;* Row 3: *box, dog, lock, mop.* Practice sentence: *I opened the lock and a fox jumped out of the box.*

Assess Use these word pairs: *hop, hope; top, tape; dog, dig; lock, lake.*

> **Pronunciation Tip**
> **short o** When you say /o/, your mouth is open and your jaw drops. Put your hand under your chin and say /o/. See, your mouth opened and your jaw dropped. In Spanish, the sound of letter *a* is similar to /o/ in English. *Examples mami/mom; mapa/mop.*

Short u   Use with page 159.

Teach Use these /u/ words: *up, bump, slump, plug.* Row 1 of page 159: *truck, plane, puppy, train.*

Practice Row 2: *bus, duck, tub, rug;* Row 3: *bus, truck, duck, sun.* Practice sentence: *A bug on a rug jumped up and landed on a pup.*

Assess Use these word pairs: *bug, bag; tub, tube; cup, cap; cub, cube.*

> **Pronunciation Tip**
> **short e** When you say /u/, your mouth is open and your tongue is down. Say /u/ again. Is your mouth open? Is your tongue down?

Name _____

Words with Short a

- **Listen** for the sound of *a* in *apple*.
- **Circle** the pictures of words that have this sound.

ROW 1

- **Look** at each picture. **Say** its name.
- **Circle** the word that names each picture.

ROW 2

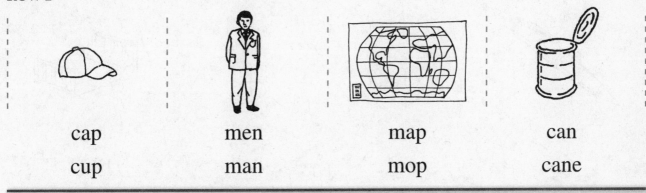

cap	men	map	can
cup	man	mop	cane

- **Look** at each picture. **Say** its name.
- **Write** the name of the picture.

ROW 3

 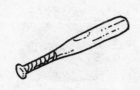 

_____ _____ _____ _____

Find short *a* in this sentence. Then **practice** chanting or singing the sentence.

The acrobat hit an apple with a bat in the middle of her act.

Name _____

Words with Short e

- **Listen** for the sound of *e* in *elbow*.
- **Circle** the pictures of words that have this sound.

ROW 1

- **Look** at each picture. **Say** its name.
- **Circle** the word that names each picture.

ROW 2

| pine | web | ball | bed |
| pen | weed | bell | bead |

- **Look** at each picture. **Say** its name.
- **Write** the name of the picture.

ROW 3

_____ _____ _____ _____

Find short *e* in this sentence. Then **practice** chanting or singing the sentence.

The elephant entered the tent with an elegant step.

Name _____

Words with Short *i*

- **Listen** for the sound of *i* in *pig*.
- **Circle** the pictures of words that have this sound.

ROW 1

 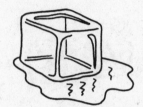 

- **Look** at each picture. **Say** its name.
- **Circle** the word that names each picture.

ROW 2

pin	zip	dog	set
pine	zap	dig	sit

- **Look** at each picture. **Say** its name.
- **Write** the name of the picture.

ROW 3

_____ _____ _____ _____

Find short *i* in this sentence. Then **practice** chanting or singing the sentence.

Six pigs with bibs grinned and did a jig in a minute.

Name _____

Words with Short o

- **Listen** for the sound of *o* in *ox*.
- **Circle** the pictures of words that have this sound.

ROW 1

   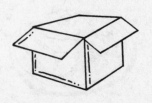

- **Look** at each picture. **Say** its name.
- **Circle** the word that names each picture.

ROW 2

lick	rock	fox	hop
lock	rack	fix	hope

- **Look** at each picture. **Say** its name.
- **Write** the name of the picture.

ROW 3

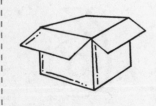  

_____ _____ _____ _____

Find short *o* in this sentence. Then **practice** chanting or singing the sentence.

I opened the lock and a fox jumped out of the box.

Name _____

Words with Short *u*

- **Listen** for the sound of *u* in *sun*.
- **Circle** the pictures of words that have this sound.

ROW 1

- **Look** at each picture. **Say** its name.
- **Circle** the word that names each picture.

ROW 2

bus	dock	tub	rug
boss	duck	tube	rag

- **Look** at each picture. **Say** its name.
- **Write** the name of the picture.

ROW 3

_____ _____ _____ _____

Find short *u* in this sentence. Then **practice** chanting or singing the sentence.

A bug on a rug jumped up and landed on a pup.

Long Vowels

Transition to English

Long vowels and the vowel digraphs that produce long vowel sounds can be confusing for English language learners. For example, some long vowel sounds in English are similar to the sounds made by different vowels or vowel combinations in Spanish. As a result, Spanish speakers may spell long *a* words with an *e*, or long *i* words with *ai*. The following lessons provide practice for hearing, producing, and spelling long vowel sounds. This model lesson gives you a pattern for teaching.

☆ Model Lesson: Long *a*   Use with page 162.

Introduce Copy and distribute page 162. Have students point to the bunch of grapes at the top of the page. Say: *These are grapes. Grapes has the sound of /ā/. Say it with me: /ā/, /ā/, grapes.* Repeat for *rain* and *tray.*

Teach Tell students: *The /ā/ sound is one sound of the letter* a. *We call this sound the long* a. *Repeat these /ā/ words after me: age, name, make, place, state.*

Ask students to name the items in Row 1 on page 162 *(cake, cat, train, whale).* Repeat each word, clearly pronouncing the vowel each time. Then say: *I'll say these words again. If you hear the /ā/ sound, circle the picture:* cake, cat, train, whale. Students should circle the *cake, train,* and *whale* pictures—but not the *cat.*

Point out that there are different ways of spelling long *a* words. Write a 3-column chart on the board with the headings *a_e, ai,* and *ay.* List the words *grapes, rain,* and *tray* in the columns where they belong. Add the long *a* words from Row 1 to the chart. Invite students to suggest other long *a* words they know that can be added to the chart.

Practice Have students look at the pictures in Row 2 on page 162. Have them read the words below each picture and circle the word that names it *(snake, chain, plane, hay).* Then have them look at the pictures in Row 3, say the name of each picture, and write the names *(grapes, tray, cake, rain).*

Read the practice sentence aloud, and have students find the long *a* words *(came, gate, cave, waited, Dave).* Invite students to chant the sentence together, clapping each time they hear long *a.*

Assess Tell students: *I will say some word pairs. Raise your hand if both words have the /ā/ sound:* sell, sale; cage, rage; ate, late; gate, get; rack, rake. Then have students repeat the word pairs after you, striving for the correct pronunciation of /ā/. Keep in mind that students who have difficulty pronouncing /ā/ may still be able to comprehend long *a* words that they hear or read.

Adapting the ☆ **Model Lesson**

Use the same lesson format above to teach the long vowels /ē/, /ī/, /ō/, and /ū/. The following information will help you to customize each lesson.

> **Pronunciation Tip**
> **long *a*** When you start to say /ā/, your mouth is open. Your tongue is in the middle of your mouth. To finish the sound /ā/, your tongue and your jaw move up a little. Try it: /ā/, /ā/, ape. The long *a* sound is similar to the Spanish digraph *ei.* Example: *rain/reina* (queen).

© Pearson Education, Inc.

Notes for Additional Lessons

Long *e*

Use with page 163.

Teach Use these /ē/ words: *bee, beaver, me, team.* Row 1 of page 163: *eagle, teeth, eye, feet.* Make a 4-column chart for long e words.

Practice Row 2: *he, wheel, thirty, leaf.* Row 3: *tree, leaf, me, bee.* Practice sentence: See the leaves on the trees on our street.

Assess Use these word pairs: *team, Tim; meat, met; leaf, lean; seen, seat; wheat, wet.*

> **Pronunciation Tip**
> **long e** *When you say /ē/, your lips are stretched wide. Your mouth has a little smile when you say /ē/. Try it: /ē/, /ē/, /ē/.* The long e sound is similar to the sound of *i* in Spanish. Examples: *need/nido* (nest); *see/sí* (yes).

Long *i*

Use with page 164.

Teach Use these /ī/ words: *kite, pie, sky, why, five.* Row 1 of page 164: *bike, night, mice, fish.* Make a 5-column chart for long i words.

Practice Row 2: *ice, child, tie, light.* Row 3: *pie, kite, light, sky.* Practice sentence: Five kites in the sky are flying high.

Assess Use these word pairs: *fight, fit; sky, sly; mice, miss; rice, price; light, lit.*

> **Pronunciation Tip**
> **long i** *When you say /ī/, your mouth is open and your jaw drops. Your tongue is down. To finish the sound /ī/, your tongue and your jaw move up. Try it: /ī/, /ī/, /ī/.* The long i sound is similar to the Spanish digraphs *ai* and *ay.* Examples: *I/hay* (there is/are); *bike/baile* (dance).

Long *o*

Use with page 165.

Teach Use these /ō/ words: *rose, goat, pillow, smoke.* Row 1 of page 165: *rope, lock, nose, bone.* Make a 4-column chart for long o words.

Practice Row 2: *robe, gold, bow, boat.* Row 3: *goat, rose, snow, gold.* Practice sentence: Joan wrote a note and rode on a boat.

Assess Use these word pairs: *boat, bought; globe, lobe; low, blow; hose, toes; coat, cot.*

> **Pronunciation Tip**
> **long o** *When you say /ō/, your mouth is round. Try it: /ō/, /ō/, /ō/.* The long o sound is similar to the sound of *o* in Spanish. Example: *no/no.*

Long *u*

Use with page 166.

Teach Use these /ū/ words: *flute, balloon, cube, use, news, true, blue.* Row 1 of page 166: *boat, boot, suitcase, foot.* Make a 5-column chart for long u words.

Practice Row 2: *glue, stool, fruit, mule.* Row 3: *fruit, flute, moon, cube.* Practice sentence: Sue used blue when she drew the moon.

Assess Use these word pairs: *tune, ton; rule, tool; soon, son; glue, blue; too, toe.*

> **Pronunciation Tip**
> **long u** *When you say /ū/ in a word like* rule, *your mouth is round and the opening is small. Try it: /ū/, /ū/. When you say /ū/ in a word like* use, *your lips start out in a line. Then they move into a circle. Try it: /ū/, /ū/.* The long u sound in *tube* is similar to the sound of *u* in Spanish: *tube/tubo.* The long u sound in *unit* is similar to the sound of *iu* or *yu* in Spanish: *unit/yugo.*

Name _____

Words with Long a

- **Listen** for the sound of *a* in *grapes*.
- **Circle** the pictures of words that have this sound.

ROW 1

- **Look** at each picture. **Say** its name.
- **Circle** the word that names each picture.

ROW 2

| snack | chin | plan | hay |
| snake | chain | plane | hat |

- **Look** at each picture. **Say** its name.
- **Write** the name of the picture.

ROW 3

_____ _____ _____ _____

Find long *a* in this sentence. Then **practice** chanting or singing the sentence.

We came to a gate by the cave and waited for Dave.

ELL and Transition Handbook

Name _____

Words with Long e

- **Listen** for the sound of *e* in *bee*.
- **Circle** the pictures of words that have this sound.

ROW 1

   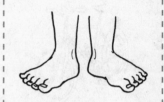

- **Look** at each picture. **Say** its name.
- **Circle** the word that names each picture.

ROW 2

he	well	thirst	leaf
hi	wheel	thirty	loaf

- **Look** at each picture. **Say** its name.
- **Write** the name of the picture.

ROW 3

Find long *e* in this sentence. Then **practice** chanting or singing the sentence.

See the leaves on the trees on our street.

Name _____

Words with Long *i*

- **Listen** for the sound of *i* in *kite*.
- **Circle** the pictures of words that have this sound.

ROW 1

- **Look** at each picture. **Say** its name.
- **Circle** the word that names each picture.

ROW 2

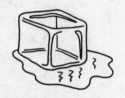  

ice	child	tie	lit
ace	chill	tea	light

- **Look** at each picture. **Say** its name.
- **Write** the name of the picture.

ROW 3

_____ _____ _____ _____

Find long *i* in this sentence. Then **practice** chanting or singing the sentence.

Five kites in the sky are flying high.

Name _____

Words with Long o

- **Listen** for the sound of *o* in *goat*.
- **Circle** the pictures of words that have this sound.

ROW 1

- **Look** at each picture. **Say** its name.
- **Circle** the word that names each picture.

ROW 2

   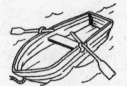

rob	gold	bow	bat
robe	good	box	boat

- **Look** at each picture. **Say** its name.
- **Write** the name of the picture.

ROW 3

_____ _____ _____ _____

Find long *o* in this sentence. Then **practice** chanting or singing the sentence.

Joan wrote a note and rode on a boat.

Words with Long *u*

- **Listen** for the sound of *u* in *flute*.
- **Circle** the pictures of words that have this sound.

ROW 1

- **Look** at each picture. **Say** its name.
- **Circle** the word that names each picture.

ROW 2

glue	stole	fright	mole
glow	stool	fruit	mule

- **Look** at each picture. **Say** its name.
- **Write** the name of the picture.

ROW 3

_____   _____   _____   _____

Find long *u* in this sentence. Then **practice** chanting or singing the sentence.

Sue used blue when she drew the moon.

Transition to English

The /r/ sound is flapped or rolled in languages such as Spanish, Polish, Farsi, and Arabic, so speakers of these languages may have difficulty pronouncing words with r-controlled vowels, especially in words such as *part* and *turn*, when r is followed by a consonant. Also, Spanish does not have a sound that is equivalent to /er/, so Spanish speakers may pronounce *bird* as *beerd* or *later* as *la-tair*. The following lessons provide practice for hearing and pronouncing words with r-controlled vowels.

Words with *ar*, *are*, *air*, *or*, *ore*
Use with page 169.

Introduce Copy and distribute page 169. Have students point to the picture of the arm at the top of the page. Say: *This is an arm. Arm has the sound of /ar/. Say it with me: /ar/, /ar/, arm.* Repeat the procedure for the sound of /air/ in the word *chair*, and the sound of /or/ in the word *horn*.

Teach Tell students: *The sound of a vowel changes when it is followed by the sound of r. We say that these kinds of vowels are r-controlled vowels. Repeat these words with* r-controlled vowels: barn, harp, jar, care, stare, air, hair, thorn, chore, more, core.

Ask students to name the items in Row 1 on page 169 *(stair, shark, car, fair)*. Repeat each word, clearly pronouncing the vowel each time. Then say: *I'll say these words again. If you hear the* r-controlled vowel sound in *arm, circle the* ar. *If you hear the* r-controlled vowel sound in *chair, circle the* air. Repeat the words one more time, pausing as you go to give students time to circle their choice. Then ask students to name the items in Row 2 *(corn, horse, car, fork)*. Repeat each word, clearly pronouncing the vowel each time. Then say: *I'll say these words again. If you hear the* r-controlled vowel sound in *horn, circle the picture.* Students should circle the pictures of the corn, horse, and fork.

Practice Have students look at the pictures in Row 3 on page 169. Have them name the pictures *(star, hair, store, porch)*. Then ask them to circle the correct word below each picture. Finally, have them write the words.

Read the practice sentence aloud, and have students find the words with r-controlled vowels (chairs, forks, corn, more, are, for, store). Invite students to chant the sentence together, clapping each time they hear the r-controlled vowels.

Assess Tell students: *I will say some words. Put your thumb up if you hear an* r-controlled vowel. *Put your thumb down if you do not:* chair, chew, chore, far, feet, stare, stand, store, car, more. Then have students repeat the r-controlled words after you, striving for the correct pronunciation of the r-controlled vowels. Keep in mind that students who have difficulty pronouncing the r-controlled vowels may still be able to comprehend words with r-controlled vowels that they hear or read.

> **Pronunciation Tip**
> *When you say words like* far, dare, *and* more, *you make the vowel sound first. Then you bring your lips together for the /r/ sound. Try:* far, dare, more.

© Pearson Education, Inc.

r-Controlled Vowels

Words with er, ir, or, ur, and eer, ear

Use with page 170.

Introduce Copy and distribute page 170. Have students point to the picture of the purse at the top of the page. Say: *This is a purse. Purse has the sound /er/. Say it with me: /er/, /er/, purse.* Repeat the procedure for the sound of /ēr/ in the word *tear.*

Teach Tell students: *The sound of a vowel changes when it is followed by the sound of r. We say that these kinds of vowels are r-controlled vowels. Repeat these words with r-controlled vowels:* fern, third, curve, dear, cheer, clear.

Ask students to name the items in Row 1 on page 170 (*nurse, ear, surf, spear*). Repeat each word, clearly pronouncing the vowel each time. Then say: *I'll say these words again. If you hear the r-controlled vowel sound in* purse, *circle the* ur. *If you hear the r-controlled vowel sound in* tear, *circle the* ear. Repeat the words one more time, pausing as you go to give students time to circle their choice.

Practice Have students look at the pictures in Row 2 on page 170 (*bird, deer, butter, skirt*) and circle the pictures of words that have the sound of -*ir* in *shirt*. Students should circle the pictures of the bird, butter, and skirt. Then have them look at the pictures in Row 3. Have them read the words below each picture, circle the correct words (*worm, deer, purse, shirt*), and write the words.

Read the practice sentence aloud, and have students find the words with *r*-controlled vowels (dear, girl, tear, purse, near, here). Invite students to chant the sentence together, clapping each time they hear the *r*-controlled vowels.

Assess Tell students: *I will say some word pairs. Raise your hand when you hear a sound with er, eer, or ear:* cheer, chair; steer, stare; her, hair; deer, door; fear, for. Then have students repeat the word pairs after you, striving for the correct pronunciation of the *r*-controlled vowels. Keep in mind that students who have difficulty pronouncing the *r*-controlled vowels may still be able to comprehend words with *r*-controlled vowels that they hear or read.

> **Pronunciation Tip**
> *When you say words like* sir *and* word, *you put your lips close together and hold them: /er/, /er/. When you say a word like* fear, *your lips start out in a line. Then you bring your lips together for the /r/ sound. Try it: / r/, /r/,* fear.

Name _____

Words with *ar, are, air, or, ore*

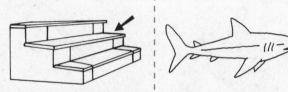

- If the word has the sound of *ar* in *arm*, **circle** the *ar*.
- If the word has the sound of *air* in *chair*, **circle** the *air*.

ROW 1

| ar | air | ar | air | ar | air | ar | air |

- If the picture has the sound of *or* in *horn*, **circle** it.

ROW 2

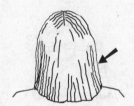

- **Look** at each picture. **Say** its name.
- **Circle** the correct word. **Write** the name of the picture.

ROW 3

| stair | hair | stare | porch |
| star | here | store | perch |

_____ _____ _____ _____

Find words with r in this sentence. Then **practice** chanting or singing the sentence.

Chairs, forks, corn, and so much more are all for sale in the store.

Name _____

Words with *er, ir, or, ur, eer, ear*

- If the word has the sound of *ur* in *purse*, **circle** the *ur*.
- If the word has the sound of *ear* in *tear*, **circle** the *ear*.

ROW 1

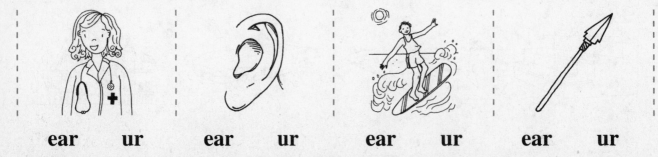

| ear | ur | ear | ur | ear | ur | ear | ur |

- If the picture has the sound of *ir* in *shirt*, **circle** it.

ROW 2

- **Look** at each picture. **Say** its name.
- **Circle** the correct word. **Write** the name of the picture.

ROW 3

| warm | deer | purse | short |
| worm | door | pass | shirt |

_____ _____ _____ _____

Find words with *r* in this sentence. Then **practice** chanting or singing the sentence.

"Oh, dear," said the girl with a tear. "My purse is not near here."

Transition to English

Some languages are "syllable-timed" languages: the syllables within words are each pronounced in the same amount of time. In English, by contrast, vowels in stressed syllables are pronounced more distinctly. Vowels in unstressed syllables often take a more neutral schwa sound. This lesson provides practice with the schwa sound, which English language learners may have difficulty pronouncing and spelling.

The Schwa and Unstressed Syllables   Use with page 172.

Introduce Copy and distribute page 172. Have students point to the picture of the pretzel. Say: *This is a pretzel. Say the two syllables of pretzel with me: PRET-zel. Which syllable sounds louder? Yes, the first syllable. It is the stressed syllable. The second syllable is the unstressed syllable, and it sounds more quiet. Look at Row 1. Listen to the vowel sound in the unstressed syllables of these words: a-LARM, a-FRAID, BOT-tle, DRAG-on. The vowel sound in the unstressed syllables sounds like this: /ə/. We call this the schwa sound. Say the schwa sound in these words: PRET-zel, a-FRAID.*

Teach Tell students: *In English, unstressed syllables often have a schwa sound. The schwa sound can be at the beginning, middle, or end of a word:* about, alone, animal, avenue, ribbon, table.

Have students look at Row 1. Repeat each word. Say: *Circle the words that have the /ə/ sound in the first syllable. Underline the words that have the /ə/ sound in the last syllable.* Read the words aloud one more time. Students should circle *alarm* and *afraid.* They should underline *bottle* and *dragon.*

Tell students: *It can be hard to know how to spell syllables that have a schwa sound, because this sound can be spelled with any vowel. It can also be spelled with a consonant + le, as in* table.

Practice Ask students to name the items in the chart on page 172 (*medal, sandal, nickel, shovel, table, apple, wagon, button*). Repeat each word and then say: *The chart shows some of the ways that the schwa sound can be spelled at the end of words. Look at each picture and write its name.*

Read the practice sentence aloud, and have students find the words with the schwa sound (*apples, bagels, alarm, a, pretzel, table*). Invite students to chant the sentence together, raising a finger each time they hear the schwa sound.

Assess Tell students: *I will say a list of words. Put your hand up when you hear a word with the /ə/ sound:* asleep, asking, final, panel, pancake, cradle, crazy, lesson, ribbon, backbone. Then have students repeat the words with a schwa sound, striving for the correct pronunciation: *asleep, final, panel, cradle, lesson,* and *ribbon.* Keep in mind that students who have difficulty pronouncing the schwa may still be able to comprehend words with /ə/ that they hear or read.

> **Pronunciation Tip**
> **schwa** *When you say the schwa sound, it sounds a little like the /u/ sound in up. But you say it quickly and without any stress on the syllable: /ə/, /ə/, /ə/. Try these words with a schwa sound:* about, around, final, little, taken, pencil, jungle, able.

© Pearson Education, Inc.

The Schwa and Unstressed Syllables

- **Say** each word. If you hear the schwa sound in the first syllable, **circle** the word.
- If you hear the schwa sound in the last syllable, **underline** the word.

ROW 1

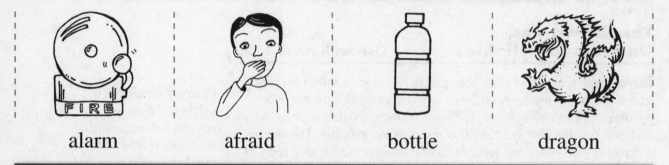

| alarm | afraid | bottle | dragon |

- **Look** at the pictures in each column. **Write** the word for each picture.

Final Syllables with Schwa			
-al	-el	-le	-on

Find words with a schwa sound in this sentence. Then **practice** chanting or singing the sentence.

There are three apples, two bagels, one alarm clock, and a pretzel on the table.

Transition to English

Inflected endings may be challenging for English language learners. For example, languages such as Chinese, Hmong, and Vietnamese do not use inflected endings to form verb tenses. Students may need help understanding that adding *-ed* to a verb indicates that the action happened in the past. Spelling changes in inflected verbs may also be difficult for English language learners to master. The following lessons provide practice with the inflected endings of nouns and verbs.

Plurals and Possessives   Use with page 175.

Introduce Write the following pair of sentences on the board, and ask students how they are different: *A chair and a table are in the room. Chairs and tables are in the room.* Students will probably notice that the nouns in the first sentence are in the singular form, whereas the nouns in the second sentence are in the plural form.

Next, write these two sentences on the board, again asking students what they notice about them: *The pen of the teacher is red. The teacher's pen is red.* Both sentences mean the same, but they use different ways to show possession, or ownership.

Teach Copy the following chart on the board, and use it to teach students how to form plurals and possessives in English.

	Rules	**Examples**
Plurals	• Add *-s* to the singular form of most nouns. • Add *-es* to words that end with *sh, ch, x, s,* and *z*. • For words that end with a consonant and *y*, change the *y* to *i* before adding *-es*.	• *boys, girls, pens, balls, teachers* • *boxes, classes, brushes, dishes* • *cities, stories, candies*
Possessives with an apostrophe	• Add an apostrophe and *s* to most singular nouns • Add an apostrophe to plural nouns that end in *s*	• Juana's idea, Kin's report, Carlos's dog • the girls' uniforms, the boys' team

Practice Copy and distribute page 175. Read the directions aloud, and direct students' attention to the pictures of the children and their pets. Have students complete the sentences by writing each word in parentheses in the plural or possessive form, as appropriate. (See answers on page 202.)

Assess Tell students to write pairs of sentences about a friend and a family member. The first sentence should introduce the person, and the second sentence tells about something that person has or owns. Write this example on the board: *My friend's name is Samuel. Samuel's wheelchair can go fast.*

Verb Endings -s, -ed, -ing   Use with page 176.

Introduce Write these verbs on the board and read them aloud for the class, asking students to pay close attention to the sound at the end of each word: *washes, cleans, writes, sleeps, fixes, plays, swims, talks.* Ask students if they noticed a difference in the way the final -s was pronounced in certain words. Confirm for them that *writes, sleeps,* and *talks* are pronounced with the sound of /s/ at the end, and that *washes, cleans, fixes, plays,* and *swims* are pronounced with the sound of /z/.

In a similar way, ask students to determine if the following words end with the sound of /d/ or /t/: *walked, enjoyed, liked, talked, played, measured.*

Finally, have students practice saying the following gerunds aloud, modeling correct pronunciation as necessary: *playing, cleaning, jogging, talking, washing, swimming.*

Teach The following rules may help students know which pronunciation to use with words that end in -s and -ed. Remind students that these are general guidelines, and that they should listen carefully to native speakers for further guidance.

For words that end in -s,
• use the sound of /s/ if the letter before it is *k, p,* or *t.*
• use the sound of /z/ if the letter before it is *b, f, g, m, n,* or a vowel.
Note: If a word ends in silent *e,* the sound of -s depends on the letter before the *e.*

For words that end in -ed,
• use the sound of /d/ if the letter before it is *b, l, m, n,* or a vowel.
• use the sound of /t/ if the letter before it is *ch, k, p, s, sh,* or *x.*

To make the -ing form of a verb,
• add -ing to the simple verb.
• double final *b, g, m, n,* or *p* before adding -ing.
• drop silent *e* before adding -ing.

Practice Copy and distribute page 176. Read the directions aloud, and have students look at the sample answers to help them get started. After students complete the activities, practice saying the verbs in each chart aloud. (See answers on page 203.)

Assess Ask students to write three sentences using a verb from each of the three charts on page 176, keeping the verb in the same form as in the chart.

Plurals and Possessives

- **Look** at the pictures. **Read** the children's names.
- **Complete** each sentence. Use the word in parentheses. Make the word possessive or plural.

Martin

Miho

Mia

Carlos

1. The children's (pet) _____ are nice and friendly.

2. (Martin) _____ lizard is very tame.

3. The (birds) _____ cage is open.

4. (Mia) _____ cat likes to sit on her lap.

5. (Carlos) _____ dog is still a puppy.

6. (Puppy) _____ like to play.

Name _____

Verb Endings -s, -ed, -ing

Part 1
• **Read** the verbs in the box.
• **Write** the -s form of the verb in the correct column of the chart.

ask	call	help	write
play	run	walk	see

/s/	/z/
asks	

Part 2
• **Read** the verbs in the box.
• **Write** the -ed form of the verb in the correct column of the chart.

call	fix	help	open
play	rub	walk	wash

/d/	/t/
called	

Part 3
• **Read** the words in the chart.
• **Write** the correct -ing form of the verb in the second column.

Verb	*-ing* Form
call	
hope	
play	
run	

ELL and Transition Handbook

Transition to English

Compound words exist in many languages, including Spanish, Vietnamese, Haitian Creole, German, and Russian. Children may readily understand the concept of compound words, but may need additional help with decoding to break English compound words into their parts. **Homophones** are also common in other languages, but English language learners may not recognize that English homophone pairs have the same pronunciation despite their different spellings. They may need to learn to use their knowledge of word meaning to choose the correct spelling of homophones. Some languages, such as the Romance languages, include **contractions**, but English language learners may need help recognizing them in English and using apostrophes correctly. The following lessons provide practice with compound words, homophones, and contractions.

Compound Words   Use with page 180.

Introduce On two separate index cards, write the words *story* and *teller*. Ask students to define each word. If necessary, define *teller* as "a person who talks or tells something" (as opposed to a teller at a bank). Then hold the cards side by side, ask students what *storyteller* means, and confirm that it means "a person who tells stories." Explain that the new word is a compound word. It is made up of two smaller words.

Teach Tell students: *When you make a compound word, you put two words together to make a new word. Usually, there isn't any change to the spelling of the two smaller words.*
   Write the following pairs of words on separate index cards: *butter, fly; milk, shake; hand, writing; sun, flower.* Discuss the meaning of each separate word, and then show how the words can be combined to create a new word. Point out that neither of the smaller words has a spelling change. The words are simply put together to create a new word. Ask students to share any other compounds that they know. Spanish examples include *abrelatas* (can opener), *rascacielos* (skyscraper), and *parasol* (parasol).

Practice Copy and distribute page 180. Read the directions aloud, and help students read the words if necessary. After students complete the activities, practice saying the compound words aloud. (See answers on page 203.)

Assess Form pairs of students, and provide partners with a set of word cards with words from page 180. Challenge students to match the cards to create a complete set of compound words. To check comprehension, ask each pair to make an oral sentence with three words from their set.

Homophones   Use with page 181.

Introduce Tell students this joke in the form of a question and answer: *What is black and white and read all over? A newspaper!* Explain to students that the question seems to be asking about colors (black, white, and red), but there is a play on the word *red*. The color red sounds the same as *read,* a past form of the verb *read*. Explain that this joke is based on a pair of homophones *(red* and *read),* two words that sound the same but are spelled differently and mean completely different things.

Teach Write the following homophone pairs on the board: *pair, pear; flour, flower; ceiling, sealing; week, weak*. Explain the meaning of each word and point out the two different spellings. Model the pronunciation, emphasizing that the two words in each pair are pronounced in exactly the same way. Invite students to share any other homophones that they know. Spanish examples include *casa/caza* (house/hunt), *hola/ola* (hello/wave), and *ciento/siento* (one hundred/I feel).

Practice Copy and distribute page 181. Read the directions aloud, and help students answer the first item in each exercise. Help students read the words if necessary. When they are finished, invite volunteers to write their answers on the board. Review the meanings of the words. Make corrections as necessary, and tell students to correct their own work as well. (See answers on page 203.)

Assess Ask students to write three sentences that include a pair of homophones, such as: *Our English class is an hour long.* Encourage students to make simple jokes with the homophones; they can also write sentences that are fanciful or silly, as in: *On Monday, I was too weak to make it through the whole week.* Alternatively, you can dictate pairs of sentences using homophones from page 181; for example: *Mo threw the ball. The ball went through the window.* Check students' work to make sure that they used the correct homophone in each sentence.

Contractions   Use with page 182.

Introduce Write the following sentences on the board, and ask students to tell you how they are different:

I am sorry for being late to class. → *I'm sorry for being late to class.*

Confirm that *I am* has been shortened to *I'm* in the second sentence. Tell students that this is a contraction. Summarize: *The pronoun* I *and the verb* am *are put together with an apostrophe to form one word,* I'm. *The letter* a *is dropped from the word* am, *and the apostrophe takes its place.*

Teach Write the following charts on the board, asking students to tell you how to write each contraction as you go:

The Verb "be"	The Verb "have"	Negatives
I am → I'm	I have → I've	has not → hasn't
You are → You're	You have → You've	have not → haven't
He is → He's	He has → He's	are not → aren't
She is → She's	She has → She's	is not → isn't
It is → It's	It has → It's	should not → shouldn't
We are → We're	We have → We've	can not → can't
They are → They're	They have → They've	will not → won't
		do not → don't
		did not → didn't

Conclude by showing how the future tense marker *will* can be shortened and connected to a pronoun using *'ll: I'll, you'll, she'll,* etc.

Practice Copy and distribute page 182. Read the directions aloud, and complete the first line together. Help students read the dialogue if necessary. After students complete the activities, have them practice the dialogue. (See answers on page 203.)

Assess Form pairs of students, and have partners create their own dialogue between a parent and child. Tell them to include a contraction in each line of dialogue. Circulate as they work to provide assistance. When they are finished, invite students to read their dialogues aloud for the class.

Compound Words

PART 1

• **Read** the compound words.
• **Draw** a line between the two words in each compound.

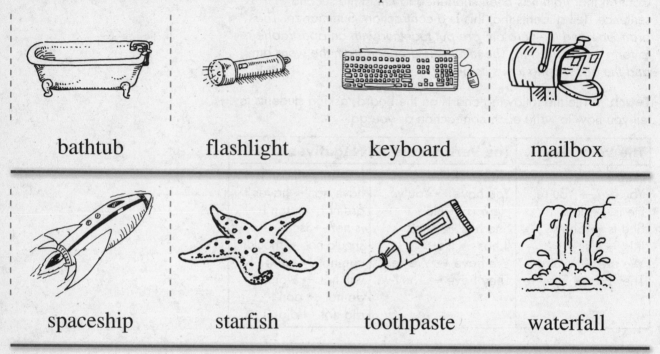

| bathtub | flashlight | keyboard | mailbox |

| spaceship | starfish | toothpaste | waterfall |

PART 2

• **Read** the two lists of words.
• **Connect** words from each list to make compounds.

back	boat
book	bow
class	brush
finger	mark
hair	nail
rain	pack
sail	room
side	walk

Name _____

Homophones

- **Read** each pair of words aloud.
- Do the words sound the same? **Check** "Same."
- Do the words sound different? **Check** "Different."

		Same	Different
1. knew	new	_____	_____
2. meal	mail	_____	_____
3. hour	our	_____	_____
4. week	weak	_____	_____
5. plate	played	_____	_____
6. best	beast	_____	_____

- **Look** at the pictures. **Read** the words aloud.
- **Draw** a line from each word to its picture.

flour

flower

tow

toe

sun

son

through

threw

© Pearson Education, Inc.

Name _____

Contractions

- **Read** the dialogue.
- **Choose** the correct word from the box to complete each sentence.
- **Write** the correct word on the blank line.

Dad: Hi, honey. Where are you going?

Grace: _____ going to soccer practice.

Dad: _____ soccer practice on Thursday night?

Grace: Yes, _____ usually on Thursday, but tonight

_____ having a special practice because of

the game on Saturday.

Dad: You finished your homework, _____ you?

Grace: _____ done my math and English. The science

teacher _____ give us homework on Wednesday.

Dad: OK. Have a good practice.

Grace: Thanks, Dad. _____ be home by six o'clock.

didn't
doesn't
I'll
I'm
I've
isn't
it's
we're

Choose four contractions. **Write** the two words that make up each one.

_____   _____   _____   _____

Transition to English

> Some English prefixes and suffixes have equivalent forms in the Romance languages. For example, the prefix *dis-* in English *(disapprove)* corresponds to the Spanish *des-* *(desaprobar)*, the French *des-* *(desapprouver)*, and the Haitian Creole *dis-* or *dez-* *(dezaprouve)*. Students who are literate in these languages may be able to transfer their understanding of prefixes and suffixes by using parallel examples in the home language and in English. Some suggestions for Spanish are provided below. The following lessons provide additional practice with prefixes and suffixes.

Prefixes *un-* and *re-*   Use with page 187.

Introduce Write these word pairs on the board: *happy, unhappy; safe, unsafe; lucky, unlucky.* Read the words aloud with students, and discuss their meanings. Ask: *What do you notice about these words?* Guide students to see that each word pair is a set of opposites, and that one word in each pair begins with *un-.* Circle the prefix *un-* in each word and say: *This syllable,* un-, *is a prefix. A prefix is a word part that is added to the beginning of a word. Adding a prefix changes the meaning of a word. A new word is made.*

Teach Present the prefixes *un-* and *re-*. Use these examples to explain how the prefixes can change the meanings of words.

Prefix	Meaning	Examples	Spanish Examples
un-	not	happy → unhappy safe → unsafe locked → unlocked	*feliz → infeliz* *seguro → inseguro*
re-	again	tell → retell do → redo write → rewrite	*contar → recontar* *hacer → rehacer*

Practice Copy and distribute page 187. Read the directions aloud, and read the first example together. Have volunteers say the words they wrote in each column of the chart. (See answers on page 203.)

Assess Have students write these prefixes and base words on cards: *un-, re-, afraid, lock, run, unite.* Have students use the cards in different combinations to make words that have prefixes. Have students show you a base word without a prefix, add a prefix, say the new word, and tell what it means.

Prefixes and Suffixes

Prefixes *im-*, *in-*, *mis-*, *over-*

Use with page 188.

Introduce Write these word pairs on the board: *patient, impatient; polite, impolite; proper, improper; pure, impure.* Read the words aloud with students, and discuss their meanings. Ask students what they notice about these words. Guide students to see that each word pair is a set of opposites, and that one word in each pair begins with *im-*. Circle the prefix *im-* in each word and explain: *This word part,* im-, *is a prefix.* It usually changes the meaning of a word to its opposite.

Teach Present the prefixes *im-*, *in-*, *mis-*, and *over-*. Use these examples to explain how the prefixes can change the meanings of words. Tell Spanish speakers that the Spanish prefixes *im-* and *in-* have similar meanings *(impaciente, intolerante)*. The Spanish prefix *sobre-* is sometimes used like the English prefix *over-* *(sobrecarga)*.

Prefix	Meaning	Examples
im-	not	*impatient, imperfect, impossible*
in-	not	*insecure, intolerant, indestructible*
mis-	wrong	*misunderstood, misbehave, mismatch*
over-	beyond, more than	*overcook, overpay, overweight*

Practice Copy and distribute page 188. Read the directions aloud, and help students fill in the first blank line. After students complete the activity, have pairs of students practice the dialogue. (See answers on page 203.)

Assess Have students write these prefixes and base words on index cards: *im-*, *in-*, *mis-*, *over-*, *correct, interpret, load, coat, take, use*. Tell students to use the cards to make words with prefixes. Circulate as they work, asking students to show you a base word and a prefix that goes with it. Ask advanced students to tell you what the word means and to use it in an oral sentence.

Suffixes -ly, -ful, -less, -ness

Use with page 189.

Introduce Write the following words on the board: *careful, carefully, careless, carelessness.* Ask students what these words have in common and what makes them different from each other. They will notice that they all have the same base, *care.* But each successive word also has a different word part at the end. Explain that each of these word parts is a *suffix.* Say: *A suffix is a word part that is added to the end of a word. Adding a suffix changes the meaning of a word.*

Teach Present the suffixes *-ly, -ful, -less,* and *-ness.* Write the following chart on the board, asking students to provide additional examples for the last column. Tell Spanish speakers that *-ly* is like the Spanish suffix *-mente.* The Spanish suffix *-dad (felicidad)* is similar to *-ness.*

Suffix	How and Why to Use It	Part of Speech	Examples
-ly	Add it to an adjective to tell how an action is done.	Adverb	*quickly* *calmly* *completely*
-ful	Add it to a noun to mean "full of" the noun.	Adjective	*thoughtful* *colorful* *helpful*
-less	Add it to a noun to mean "without" the noun.	Adjective	*spotless* *joyless* *flawless*
-ness	Add it to an adjective to describe a state of being.	Noun	*darkness* *happiness* *carelessness* *peacefulness*

Practice Copy and distribute page 189. Read the directions aloud, and have students look at the sample answer to help them get started. After students complete the activity, invite volunteers to take turns reading the passage aloud. (See answers on page 203.)

Assess Have students write these suffixes and base words on index cards: *-ly, -ful, -less, -ness, slow, quiet, perfect, fear, rude.* Tell students to use the cards to make words with suffixes. Circulate as they work, asking students to show you a base word and a suffix that goes with it. Ask advanced students to tell you what the word means and to use it in an oral sentence.

Suffixes *-tion, -sion, -able, -ible*
Use with page 190.

Introduce Write the following words on the board: *perfection, decision, walkable, sensible.* Tell students that each of these words is made up of a base word and a suffix. Circle the suffix *-tion* in the first word and explain: *This word part, -tion, is a suffix.* Ask volunteers to find the suffixes in the other three words. Point out that the base word might need a spelling change before the suffix is added. The word *decide,* for example, drops the final *-de* before adding *-sion.* The reason for these spelling changes has to do with pronunciation, and the rules are hard to generalize, as there are many exceptions to the rules. Students will learn the different spellings with practice.

Teach Present the suffixes *-tion, -sion, -able,* and *-ible.* Explain that *-tion* and *-sion* have the same meaning, as do *-able* and *-ible.* Write the following chart on the board, asking students to provide additional examples for the last column. Spanish examples of these suffixes are *-ción (reacción), -sión (decisión), -able (confortable),* and *-ible (sensible).*

Suffix	How and Why to Use It	Part of Speech	Examples
-tion, -sion	Add it to a verb to describe an action or a state of being.	Noun	*perfection imagination reaction decision admission confusion*
-able, -ible	Add it to a verb to add the meaning "can be."	Adjective	*walkable comfortable dependable sensible reversible flexible*

Practice Copy and distribute page 190. Read the directions aloud, and do the first example together. Tell students that they can use the chart on the board to check spellings. After students complete the activity, review the answers together. (See answers on page 203.)

Assess Have students write these suffixes and base words on index cards: *-tion, -sion, -able, -ible, sense, comfort, confuse, react.* Tell students to use the cards to make words with suffixes. Circulate as they work, asking students to show you a base word and a suffix that goes with it. Ask advanced students to tell you what the word means and to use it in an oral sentence.

© Pearson Education, Inc.

Name _____

Prefixes *un-* and *re-*

- **Read** each group of words.
- **Use** *un-* or *re-* to make one new word.
- **Write** the new word.

1. read again   reread _____

2. appear again   _____

3. not believable   _____

4. not familiar   _____

5. heat again   _____

6. not interested   _____

7. not like   _____

8. start again   _____

9. use again   _____

10. not kind   _____

- **Write** all the new words in the chart.

un-	re-

Prefixes *im-*, *in-*, *mis-*, *over-*

- **Read** the conversation. **Finish** the sentences with words from the box.
- Then **practice** the conversation.

Alex: This game costs too much. It is _____.
(1)

Tanya: This ball doesn't cost too much. It is _____.
(2)

Alex: The price on that sign is wrong. It is not correct.

Tanya: You're right! The price must be _____.
(3)

Alex: Let's tell someone that the sign has a _____.
Then they can fix the sign.   (4)

Tanya: OK, but let's hurry. I want to go.

Alex: Why are you so _____? We have a lot of time!
(5)

| impatient |
| incorrect |
| inexpensive |
| misprint |
| overpriced |

Write one more word for each prefix. You may use a dictionary to find the words.

im-   in-   mis-   over-

_____   _____   _____   _____

Name _____

Suffixes -*ly*, -*ful*, -*less*, -*ness*

- **Read** the story.
- **Add** -*ly, -ful, -less,* or -*ness* to each word in parentheses.

Yesterday I took Domingo, my dog, to my grandmother's house. As usual, her

house was _____spotless_____ (spot). We had milk and cookies in the kitchen while

Domingo sat _____ (quiet) in the living room. In fact, he was *too* quiet.
        (1)

I went to check on him. He had _____ (complete) chewed a pillow into
                    (2)

bits and pieces. There were feathers everywhere!

My grandmother came in the room and said, "Oh my _____!" (good)
                                (3)

"I'm sorry grandma," I said. "I should have been more _____." (care)
                                    (4)

_____ (lucky) for me, my grandmother has a good sense of humor.
    (5)

She _____ (playful) threw a pillow at me and we had a pillow fight. We
    (6)

had so much fun it was easy to forget Domingo's _____. (frisky)
                                (7)

Suffixes -*tion*, -*sion*, -*able*, -*ible*

- **Read** the sentences. **Look** at the underlined word.
- **Add** -*tion*, -*sion*, -*able*, or -*ible* to make a new word. **Write** the word.

1.

   Yasmin <u>imagined</u> being a princess.

   She used her _____.

2.

   We can <u>walk</u> on this path.

   The path is _____.

3.

   I can <u>depend</u> on Pablo.

   Pablo is _____.

4.

   Aisha <u>decided</u> which book to read.

   She made a _____.

5.

   I can <u>reverse</u> this shirt.

   The shirt is _____.

© Pearson Education, Inc.

Transition to English

> **Cognates** are words that share origins and appear in similar forms in different languages. For example, the English word *school* is of Greek origin, and it is similar to the Spanish *escuela*, the French *école*, the Polish *szkoła*, and the German *Schule*. For speakers of languages that share word origins with English, the study of cognates can be a powerful vocabulary-building tool. The following lessons provide practice for working with cognates and words with Greek and Latin roots.

Cognates   Use with page 196.

Introduce Present a chart like the one below. Read the words with students, and note the similarities across various languages. Tell students that when words look similar and have a similar meaning in different languages, they are called *cognates*. Invite students to suggest other cognates they know in English and another language. Tell students that cognates can help them understand more words in English.

English	Spanish	French	Haitian Creole	Polish
telephone	teléfono	téléphone	telefonn	telefon

> Use this lesson with students who are literate in languages that have many cognates of English words, such as Spanish, Portuguese, French, and, to a lesser extent, Haitian Creole, Polish, and Russian.

Teach Explain to students that cognates in different languages usually have the same origins. For example, the different words for *telephone* are all based on the Greek word parts *telē*, which means far off, and *phōnē*, which means sound or voice. Explain that because many scientific words have Greek or Latin origins, they often are cognates.

 Then point out that sometimes words in different languages are "false friends"—they look almost the same, but they don't mean the same thing. For example, the Spanish word *sopa* looks and sounds similar to the English word *soap*, but it means *soup*. Ask students to give other examples of "false friends," words that are not cognates.

Practice Copy and distribute page 196. Have students look for English cognates of home-language words in an English text they are currently reading. (A nonfiction science or social studies text is likely to offer more examples.) Help them decide whether or not the words really are cognates. Suggest that students consult resources such as bilingual dictionaries, other students, or the Internet (with your guidance) to find translations and word meanings. Students might make a class chart showing words for *computer* in various languages. (See answers on page 203.)

Assess Ask students to say or write five examples of cognate pairs in English and their home language, and one example of "false friends."

© Pearson Education, Inc.

Words with Greek Roots   Use with page 197.

Introduce Write the following words on the board: *autograph, phonograph, photograph, paragraph*. Ask students what all these words have in common. Confirm for them that they all have the word part *graph*. Tell students that this word part comes from the Greek language. It means "written." Conclude by saying: *Many other words in English have Greek roots, too. Learning these roots can help you learn more words.*

Teach Write the following chart on the board, asking students to provide additional examples for the last column.

Greek Root	Meaning	Sample Words
biblio	book	bibliography
bio	life	biography
crac, crat	rule, govern	democrat
demos	people	democracy
geo	earth	geology
graph, gram	written, drawn, describe, record	photograph
log	idea, word, speech, study	biology
meter	measure	perimeter
phono	sound	symphony
scope	to see	telescope

Show students how different word parts can be combined. The root *bio*, for example, can be combined with *graph* to form *biography*, and it can also be combined with *logy* to form *biology*. Knowing this, students can conclude that any word with the root *bio* has to do with life. Tell Spanish speakers that many Spanish words have these same Greek roots. Ask them to provide translations for the sample words in the chart (*bibliografía, biografía, demócrata, democracia, geología, fotografía, biología, perímetro, sinfonía, telescopio*).

Practice Copy and distribute page 197. Read the directions aloud, and have students look at the sample answer to help them get started. After students complete the activity, invite volunteers to take turns forming other words with the Greek roots in the word box. (See answers on page 203.)

Assess Write the following words on the board: *autobiography, phonology, geography,* and *telescope*. Ask students to copy these words and to write their definitions, based on what they've learned. When they've finished, have a volunteer write his or her answers on the board, and model corrections as necessary. You can collect students' work for later assessment.

Words with Latin Roots   Use with page 198.

Introduce Write the following words on the board: *animal, animation, animated.* Ask students what all these words have in common. Confirm for them that they all have the word part *anima.* Tell students that this word part is from Latin, an ancient language that was originally spoken in Italy. *Anima* means "living." Conclude by saying: *Many other words in English have Latin roots, too. Learning these roots can help you learn more words.*

Teach Write the following chart on the board, asking students to provide additional examples for the last column. Tell Spanish speakers that Spanish comes from Latin, so these roots should be familiar.

Latin Root	Meaning	Sample Words
aqua	water	aquarium
aud	to hear	auditorium
cent	one hundred	century
cert	sure, to trust	certificate
circ	around	circle
compute	to compute	computer
dic, dict	to say, to speak	dictionary
fin	to end	finish
grad	step, degree	graduate
scrib	to write	scribble

Practice Copy and distribute page 198. Read the directions aloud, and have students look at the sample answer to help them get started. After students complete the activity, invite volunteers to take turns forming other words with the Latin roots in the answer box. (See answers on page 204.)

Assess Write the following words on the board: *certain, final, audition, gradual,* and *dictate.* Ask students to copy these words and to identify their Latin roots. To check comprehension, ask students to make a sentence with each of these words.

Related Words   **Use with page 199.**

Introduce On the board, write *breath, breathe,* and *breathless.* Ask students what these words have in common. Confirm for them that they all have the word *breath* as the base. The endings on the other two words change their part of speech and meaning. *Breathe* is a verb and *breathless* is an adjective. Many other words are closely related in the same way. Tell students that it will help them expand their vocabulary if they try to learn new words in groups with other related words.

Teach Write the following chart on the board, asking students to provide additional examples for the last column. Spanish examples include *planeta/planetario, horizonte/horizontal,* and *salud/saludable.*

Base Word	Related Words
jewel	jeweler, jewelry
planet	planetary, planetarium
paint	painter, painting
act	action, actor, active
sign	signature
compute	computer, computation
horizon	horizontal
pot	potter, pottery
bank	banker, banking
heal	health, healthy
relate	relative, relationship
produce	product, production
please	pleasant, pleasure

Practice Copy and distribute page 199. Read the directions aloud, and have students look at the sample answer to help them get started. (See answers on page 204.)

Assess Ask students to take turns thinking of other words that are related to the words in the word box on page 199 or the words in the above chart.

Reading Multisyllabic Words

Use with page 200.

Introduce On the board, write the word *dic/tion/ar/y*, dividing it into syllables, as indicated. Sound it out, pausing between each syllable, and then blend the syllables together. Ask students how many syllables it has (4). Follow the same procedure for *en/cy/clo/pe/di/a*, which has 6 syllables. Tell students: *Pay attention to the syllables in a word. This will help you spell the word, and it will help you pronounce it, too.*

Teach Distribute multiple copies of a dictionary, and point out how each entry word is divided into syllables. Ask students to find the word *brontosaur*, for example. Ask: *How many syllables does this word have?* (3) *What's the first syllable?* (bron) *What are the other syllables?* (*to* and *saur*) Repeat the procedure with the following words: *mystery, parentheses, enthusiasm, personality.*

Practice Copy and distribute page 200. Read the directions aloud, and have students look at the sample answer to help them get started. Help students read the words if necessary. (See answers on page 204.)

Assess Write the following words on the board: *relative, warrior, mathematical, magnificent, principal.* Have students use a dictionary to find out how many syllables each word has. Tell students to write the words on a piece of paper, showing the syllable divisions.

Cognates

- **Read** a few pages of a book or article. **Find** English words that look like words in another language you know.
- **Write** the words in both languages on the chart.
- **Write** the meaning of each word, using dictionaries if necessary. Then tell if the two similar words are cognates.

English	_____ (language)	Cognates? (yes/no)
Word: **Meaning:**	**Word:** **Meaning:**	
Word: **Meaning:**	**Word:** **Meaning:**	
Word: **Meaning:**	**Word:** **Meaning:**	
Word: **Meaning:**	**Word:** **Meaning:**	
Word: **Meaning:**	**Word:** **Meaning:**	

- **Find out** how to say *computer* in at least two different languages. **Use** sources such as dictionaries, the Internet, and people you know. **Write** the words.
- **Decide** which words are cognates of *computer.*

© Pearson Education, Inc.

Name _____

Words with Greek Roots

- **Read** the word parts in the box.
- **Look** at the pictures. Put the word parts together to make words.
- **Write** the correct word on each blank line.

auto = self	**micro** = very small	**scope** = to see
graph = written	**phone/phono** = sound	**tele** = from a distance
mega = large	**photo** = light	

1. 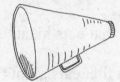 _____megaphone_____ = a tool used to make sound "larger"

2. 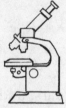 _____ = a tool for seeing very small things

3.  _____ = a machine that allows two people in different places to talk

4.  _____ = a person's signature

5.  _____ = a tool for seeing the planets and stars

6.  _____ = an image taken by a camera

Name _____

Words with Latin Roots

- **Study** the word parts in the box.
- **Read** the sentences.
- **Complete** each sentence. **Write** the correct word in the blank space.

aqua = water	**herba** = plant	**terr** = earth
carn = meat	**mill** = thousand	**tract** = pull
cent = one hundred	**project** = throw	

1.  A _____carnivore_____ is an animal that eats meat, and

an _____ is an animal that eats plants.

(herbivore, carnivore)

2.  A _____ is one hundred years, and a

_____ is one thousand years.

(century, millenium)

3. 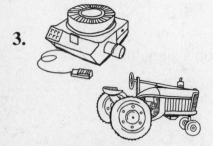 A _____ is a machine that "throws light,"

and a _____ is a machine that pulls heavy

loads. (tractor, projector)

4. 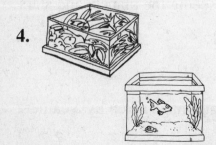 Small plants are grown in a _____, and

fish are kept in an _____.

(terrarium, aquarium)

Related Words

- **Look** at the words in the box.
- **Read** the sentences.
- **Complete** each sentence. **Write** the correct word in the blank space.

desert	dirt	mask	painter	volcanic
deserted	dirty	masquerade	painting	volcano

1.

The _____volcano_____ exploded with a huge blast.

_____ ash rose into the air and then

settled on the ground.

2.

The _____ is finishing a pretty

_____.

3.

This part of the _____ is quiet

and _____.

4.

Everybody at the _____ wore a

_____.

5.

After playing in the _____ all day long,

Cory's shirt was completely _____.

© Pearson Education, Inc.

Reading Multisyllabic Words

- **Read** the words. Sound out the number of syllables.
- **Write** each word in the correct column of the chart.

ROW 1

         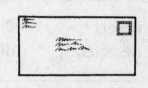

baseball   binoculars   champion   envelope

ROW 2

mushroom   pineapple   watermelon   meditation

ROW 3

   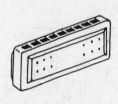      

barbecue   harmonica   telescope   zipper

Two Syllables	Three Syllables	Four Syllables
baseball		

pages 140–142:
Confusing Consonants, Assess
b and *v*: b, v, b, v, v, b, v, b, b, v, b, v, v
ch and *sh*: ch, sh, ch, sh, ch, ch, sh, sh, ch, ch, sh
d and *th*: th, d, th, th, d, d, th, d, th, d
l and *r*: r, l, r, l, r, r, l, r, l, r, l, l
m and *n*: m, n, m, n, m, n, m, n, n, m, m, n
s and *th*: s, th, s, th, s, s, th, th, s, th

page 143: Words with *b* and *v*
Row 1: b, v, b, v
Row 2: v, v, b, b
Row 3: box, van
Sentence: Val, Billy, dove, wave

page 144: Words with *ch* and *sh*
Row 1: sh, ch, ch, sh
Row 2: sh, sh, ch, ch
Row 3: child, shop
Sentence: Sherry, Shark, chewed, shiny, shoe

page 145: Words with *d* and *th*
Row 1: d, th, th, d
Row 2: th, th, d, d
Row 3: third, desk
Sentence: Think, thought, daring, dog, through, thick

page 146: Words with *l* and *r*
Row 1: r, l, l, r
Row 2: r, l, l, r
Row 3: leg, ring
Sentence: red, river, runs, little, lake

page 147: Words with *m* and *n*
Row 1: n, n, m, m
Row 2: m, n, m, n
Row 3: mask, nest
Sentence: man, in, moon, cream, spoon

page 148: Words with *s* and *th*
Row 1: s, th, th, s
Row 2: s, s, th, th
Row 3: sun, thorn
Sentence: Sara, sipped, thick, soup

pages 149–150:
Consonant Blends, Assess
Initial Consonant Blends: cr, pl, cl, pr, tr, str, dr, st
Final Consonant Blends: nk, nch, nk, nd, nch, nk, sk, st, nt, nd, nt, nd

page 151: Initial Consonant Blends
Row 1: cr, cr, cl, cl
Row 2: pr, pl, pr, pl
Row 3: str, str, st, st
Sentence: clock, struck, students, snapped

page 152: Final Consonant Blends
Row 1: nd, nk, nd, nk
Row 2: nt, nt, nch, nch
Row 3: sk, st, st, sk
Sentence: must, ask, band, paint, bench

pages 153–154:
Short Vowels, Assess
Short *a*: pat, hat, bad, man, tag
Short *e*: set, ten, net, sell
Short *i*: tin, six, pig, trip
Short *o*: hop, top, dog, lock
Short *u*: bug, tub, cup, cub

page 155: Words with Short *a*
Row 1: acrobat, bat, ant
Row 2: cap, man, map, can
Row 3: man, bat, ant, hat
Sentence: acrobat, an, apple, bat, act

page 156: Words with Short *e*
Row 1: vest, elephant, tent
Row 2: pen, web, bell, bed
Row 3: ten, bell, nest, web
Sentence: elephant, entered, tent, elegant, step

page 157: Words with Short *i*
Row 1: dinner, gift, inch
Row 2: pin, zip, dig, sit
Row 3: zip, gift, pig, six
Sentence: Six, pigs, with, bibs, grinned, did, jig, in, minute

page 158: Words with Short o
Row 1: dog, octopus, box
Row 2: lock, rock, fox, hop
Row 3: box, dog, lock, mop
Sentence: lock, fox, box

page 159: Words with Short u
Row 1: truck, puppy
Row 2: bus, duck, tub, rug
Row 3: bus, truck, duck, sun
Sentence: bug, rug, jumped, up, pup

pages 160–161:
Long Vowels, Assess
Long *a*: cage, rage; ate, late
Long *e*: leaf, lean; seen, seat
Long *i*: sky, sly; rice, price
Long *o*: globe, lobe; low, blow; hose, toes
Long *u*: rule, tool; glue, blue

page 162: Words with Long a
Row 1: cake, train, whale
Row 2: snake, chain, plane, hay
Row 3: grapes, tray, cake, rain
Sentence: came, (a), gate, cave, waited, Dave

page 163: Words with Long e
Row 1: eagle, teeth, feet
Row 2: he, wheel, thirty, leaf
Row 3: tree, leaf, me, bee
Sentence: See, leaves, trees, street

page 164: Words with Long i
Row 1: bike, night, mice
Row 2: ice, child, tie, light
Row 3: pie, kite, light, sky
Sentence: Five, kites, sky, flying, high

page 165: Words with Long o
Row 1: rope, nose, bone
Row 2: robe, gold, bow, boat
Row 3: goat, rose, snow(man), gold
Sentence: Joan, wrote, note, rode, boat

page 166: Words with Long u
Row 1: boot, suitcase
Row 2: glue, stool, fruit, mule
Row 3: fruit, flute, moon, cube
Sentence: Sue, blue, drew, moon

pages 167–168:
r-Controlled Vowels, Assess
Words with *ar, are, air, or, ore*: thumbs up: chair, chore, far, stare, store, car, more; thumbs down: chew, feet, stand
Words with *er, ir, or, ur*, and *eer, ear*: cheer, steer, her, deer, fear

page 169:
Words with ar, are, air, or, ore
Row 1: air, ar, ar, air
Row 2: corn, horse, fork
Row 3: star, hair, store, porch
Sentence: Chairs, forks, corn, more, are, for, store

page 170:
Words with er, ir, or, ur, eer, ear
Row 1: ur, ear, ur, ear
Row 2: bird, butter, skirt
Row 3: worm, deer, purse, shirt
Sentence: dear, girl, tear, purse, near, here

page 171: The Schwa and Unstressed Syllables, Assess
asleep, final, panel, cradle, lesson, ribbon

page 172:
The Schwa and Unstressed Syllables
Row 1: circle alarm, afraid; underline bottle, dragon
Chart: medal, nickel, table, wagon, sandal, shovel, apple, button
Sentence: apples, bagels, alarm, (a), pretzel, table

pages 173–174:
Inflected Endings, Assess
Plurals and Possessives: Answers will vary, but will include possessives.
Verb Endings *-s, -ed, -ing*: Answers will vary.

page 175: Plurals and Possessives
1. pets; 2. Martin's; 3. birds'; 4. Mia's;
5. Carlos's; 6. Puppies

page 176: Verb Endings -s, -ed, -ing
/s/: helps, writes, walks; /z/: calls, plays, runs, sees
/d/: opened, played, rubbed; /t/: fixed, helped, walked, washed
-ing Form: calling, hoping, playing, running

pages 177–179:
Compound Words, Homophones, and Contractions, Assess
Compound Words: Answers may include any of the words on page 180.
Homophones: Answers will vary.
Contractions: Answers will vary.

page 180: Compound Words
Part 1: bath/tub; flash/light; key/board; mail/box; space/ship; star/fish; tooth/paste; water/fall
Part 2: backpack, bookmark, classroom, fingernail, hairbrush, rainbow, sailboat, sidewalk

page 181: Homophones
1. same; 2. different; 3. same; 4. same;
5. different; 6. different
Students will match pictures to words.

page 182: Contractions
I'm, Isn't, it's, we're, didn't, I've, doesn't, I'll
Answers will vary, but will be four of the following: did not, does not, I will, I am, I have, is not, it is, and we are.

pages 183–186: Prefixes and Suffixes, Assess
Prefixes un- and re-: unafraid, not afraid; unlock, open the lock; rerun, run again; reunite, unite again
Prefixes im-, in-, mis-, over-: incorrect, misinterpret, overload, overcoat, intake, mistake, overtake, misuse, overuse
Suffixes -ly, -ful, -less, -ness: slowly, slowness, quietly, quietness, perfectly, fearful, fearless, rudely, rudeness
Suffixes -tion, -sion, -able, -ible: sensible, comfortable, confusion, reaction

page 187: Prefixes un- and re-
2. reappear; 3. unbelievable; 4. unfamiliar;
5. reheat; 6. uninterested; 7. unlike; 8. restart;
9. reuse; 10. unkind
un-: unbelievable, unfamiliar, uninterested, unlike, unkind; re-: reread, reappear, reheat, restart, reuse

page 188: Prefixes im-, in-, mis-, over-
1. overpriced; 2. inexpensive; 3. incorrect;
4. misprint; 5. impatient
Additional words: Answers will vary. Words may include impolite, insecure, mismatch, and overcook.

page 189: Suffixes -ly, -ful, -less, -ness
quietly; completely; goodness; careful; luckily; playfully; friskiness

page 190:
Suffixes -tion, -sion, -able, -ible
1. imagination; 2. walkable; 3. dependable;
4. decision; 5. reversible

pages 191–195: Cognates and Word Roots, Assess
Cognates: Answers will vary.
Words with Greek Roots: autobiography: a book about yourself; phonology: the study of sounds; geography: description of the Earth; telescope: something that lets you see far away
Words with Latin Roots: certain, cert; final, fin; audition, aud; gradual, grad; dictate, dict
Related Words: Answers will vary.
Reading Multisyllabic Words: Syllabication may vary among dictionaries. rel/a/tive; war/rior; math/e/mat/i/cal; mag/ni/fi/cent; prin/ci/pal

page 196: Cognates
Chart: Answers will vary. The Spanish word for computer, computadora, is a cognate.

page 197: Words with Greek Roots
2. microscope; 3. telephone; 4. autograph;
5. telescope; 6. photograph

page 198: Words with Latin Roots
1. carnivore, herbivore; 2. century, millennium;
3. projector, tractor; 4. terrarium, aquarium

page 199: Related Words
1. volcano, Volcanic; 2. painter, painting;
3. desert, deserted; 4. masquerade, mask;
5. dirt, dirty

page 200: Reading Multisyllabic Words
Two Syllables: baseball, mushroom, zipper;
Three Syllables: champion, envelope, pineapple,
barbecue, telescope; Four Syllables: binoculars,
watermelon, meditation, harmonica

Professional Resources
for teachers of English Language Learners

Books and Articles

Research and Practice

Antunez, Beth. "Implementing Reading First with English Language Learners." *Directions in Language and Education,* no. 15 (Spring 2002). Published by the National Clearinghouse for English Language Acquisition and Language Instruction Educational Programs.

Cary, Stephen. *Working with Second Language Learners: Answers to Teachers' Top Ten Questions.* Heinemann, 2000.

Coelho, Elizabeth. *Adding English: A Guide to Teaching in Multilingual Classrooms.* Pippin Publishing, 2004.

Cummins, Jim. *An Introductory Reader to the Writings of Jim Cummins.* Bilingual Education and Bilingualism 29. Edited by Colin Baker and Nancy H. Hornberger. Multilingual Matters LTD, 2001.

Echevarria, Jana, MaryEllen Vogt, and Deborah J. Short. *Making Content Comprehensible for English Learners: The SIOP Model,* 2d ed. Allyn & Bacon, 2004.

Echevarria, Jana, and Anne Graves. *Sheltered Content Instruction: Teaching English-Language Learners with Diverse Abilities,* 2d ed. Allyn & Bacon, 2003.

Fay, Kathleen, and Suzanne Whaley. *Becoming One Community: Reading and Writing with English Language Learners.* Stenhouse Publishers, 2004.

Fillmore, Lily Wong. "Language in Education," in *Language in the USA: Themes for the Twenty-first Century.* Edited by Edward Finegan and John R. Rickford. Cambridge University Press, 2004, pp. 339–360.

Fillmore, Lily Wong, and Catherine E. Snow. "What Teachers Need to Know About Language." Office of Educational Research and Improvement, U.S. Department of Education, 2000.

García, Georgia Earnest. "The Selection and Use of English Texts with Young English Language Learners" in *The Texts in Elementary Classrooms.* Center for the Improvement of Early Reading Achievement (CIERA) Series. Edited by James V. Hoffman and Diane L. Schallert. Lawrence Erlbaum Associates, 2004.

García, Georgia Earnest. "The Reading Comprehension Development and Instruction of English-Language Learners," in *Rethinking Reading Comprehension.* Edited by Anne Polselli Sweet and Catherine E. Snow. The Guilford Press, 2003.

Helman, Lori A. "Building on the Sound System of Spanish: Insights from the Alphabetic Spellings of English-language Learners." *The Reading Teacher,* vol. 57, no. 5 (February 2004), pp. 452–460.

Jesness, Jerry. *Teaching English Language Learners K–12: A Quick-Start Guide for the New Teacher.* Corwin Press, 2004.

Ovando, Carlos J., Virginia P. Collier, and Mary Carol Combs. *Bilingual and ESL Classrooms: Teaching in Multicultural Contexts,* 3rd ed. McGraw Hill, 2003.

Schecter, Sandra R. and Jim Cummins, editors. *Multilingual Education in Practice: Using Diversity as a Resource.* Heinemann, 2003.

Short, Deborah J., and Jana Echevarria. (2005). "Teacher Skills to Support English Language Learners." *Educational Leadership: Educating English Language Learners,* 62(4), 8-13. Available online: http://www.ahsaa.net/archives/TeacherSkills.htm

Short, Deborah J., and Jana Echevarria. (1999, December). *The Sheltered Instruction Observation Protocol: A Tool for Teacher-researcher Collaboration and Professional Development* (ERIC Digest No. EDO-FL-99-09). Washington, DC: ERIC Clearinghouse on Languages & Linguistics. (ERIC Document Reproduction Service No. ED 436 981). Available online: http://www.cal.org/resources/digest/sheltered.html

Standards and Assessment

Bielenberg, Brian, and Lily Wong Fillmore. "The English They Need for the Test." *Educational Leadership,* vol. 62, no. 4 (December 2004/January 2005), pp. 45–49.

García, Georgia Earnest. "Assessing the Literacy Development of Second-Language Students: A Focus on Authentic Assessment," in *Kids Come in All Languages: Reading Instruction for ESL Students.* Edited by Karen Spangenberg-Urbschat and Robert Pritchard. International Reading Association, 1994, pp. 180–205.

Lachat, Mary Ann. *Standards-Based Instruction and Assessment for English Language Learners.* Corwin Press, 2004.

Teachers of English to Speakers of Other Languages, Inc. (TESOL). *Pre-K–12 English Language Proficiency Standards in the Core Content Areas.* TESOL, 2006.

Valdez-Pierce, Lorraine. *Assessing English Language Learners.* National Education Association, 2003.

Language Resources

Kaufman, Dorothy and Gary Apple. *The Oxford Picture Dictionary for the Content Areas.* Oxford University Press, 2000. Offers visual support for content-area vocabulary.

Kress, Jacqueline E. *The ESL Teacher's Book of Lists.* Jossey-Bass, 1993. Provides useful word lists, including classroom vocabulary, content-area words, and cognates in Spanish, French, and German.

Longman English/Spanish-English Dictionary for Schools. Pearson Education, 2003.

Steiner, Roger, ed. *Webster's New World® International Spanish Dictionary English/Spanish Spanish/English,* 2d ed. Wiley Publishing, Inc., 2004. A comprehensive bilingual dictionary that includes technical vocabulary, idioms, and regionalisms.

Swan, Michael and Bernard Smith, eds. *Learner English,* 2d ed. Cambridge University Press, 2001. A practical reference guide to the phonics and grammar of more than 23 world languages, including Spanish, Chinese, Korean, Arabic, Polish, Russian, and Turkish.

Professional Organizations

Association for Supervision and Curriculum Development (ASCD). Periodicals include *Educational Leadership* and *Education Update.* www.ascd.org

International Reading Association (IRA). Periodicals include *The Reading Teacher, Reading Research Quarterly, Journal of Adolescent and Adult Literacy, Lectura y vida,* and *Reading Online.* www.reading.org

National Association for Bilingual Education (NABE). Publishes the *NABE News Magazine* and the *Bilingual Research Journal,* as well as the online *NABE News Digest* and *NABE News Online.* www.nabe.org

National Association for the Education of Young Children (NAEYC). Publishes the scholarly journal *Early Childhood Research Quarterly,* the practitioner-oriented journal *Young Children,* and related books, videos, brochures, and posters. www.naeyc.org

Teachers of English to Speakers of Other Languages (TESOL). Publishes the print journal *Essential Teacher* as well as *Compleat Links,* an online complement to *Essential Teacher,* and *TESOL Connections,* a periodic e-newsletter. (Also see Standards and Assessment on page 207.) www.tesol.org

Web Sites

Research and Practice

August, Diane, and Kenji Hakuta, eds. (1997). *Improving Schooling for Language Minority Children: A Research Agenda*. National Academy Press. Available: http://books.nap. edu/books/0309054974/html/index.html

Bilingual Research Journal Online. http://brj.asu.edu

Center for Applied Linguistics (CAL). Information about languages, teaching, culture, and literacy (including the National Literacy Panel). http://www.cal.org

Center for Research on Education, Diversity, and Excellence (CREDE) http://www.crede. ucsc.edu

Crandall, Joanne, Ann Jaramillo , Laurie Olsen, and Joy Kreeft Peyton. (2002). *Using Cognitive Strategies to Develop English Language and Literacy*. ERIC Clearinghouse on Languages and Linguistics. For ordering information, see Digest Series 2 at: http://www.cal.org/resources/update.html

ESCORT (formerly Eastern Stream Center on Resources and Training) Resources for use with migrant children and other English language learners. http://www.escort.org

National Clearinghouse for English Language Acquisition and Language Instruction Educational Programs (NCELA) http://www. ncela.gwu.edu

Project More. Information for K-12 mainstream and ESL teachers. http://education.uncc.edu/ more/

SIOP Institute (Sheltered Instruction Observation Protocol).http://www.siopinstitute.net/index. html

Slavin, Robert E. and Alan Cheung. (2003). *Effective Reading Programs for English Language learners: A Best-Evidence Synthesis*. Center for Research on the Education of Students Placed at Risk, John Hopkins University. For information: www.csos.jhu.edu

Snow, Catherine E., M. Susan Burns, and Peg Griffin, eds. (1998). *Preventing Reading Difficulties in Young Children*. National Academy Press. For information: http://books. nap.edu

Thomas, Wayne P. and Virginia P. Collier. (2002). *A National Study of School Effectiveness for Language Minority Students' Long-term Academic Achievement*. Center for Research on Education, Diversity & Excellence (CREDE). Available: http:// www.crede.org/research/llaa/1.1_es.html

Standards and Assessment

Center for Advanced Research on Language Acquisition (CARLA) Bibliography: Assessment of Language Minority Students' Language and Academic Proficiency. http://www.carla.umn.edu/esl/teamup/ assessmentbib.html

Teaching Diverse Learners Web site, by the Northeast and Islands Regional Educational Laboratory (LAB) at Brown University. Assessment for English Language Learners. http://www.lab.brown.edu/tdl/assessment/ index.shtml

TESOL. *Pre-K–12 English Language Proficiency Standards in the Core Content Areas*. http://www.tesol.org

Technology

Leloup, Jean W., and Robert Ponterio. (2000). "Enhancing Authentic Language Learning Experiences Through Internet Technology." *ERIC Digest*. Available: http://www.cal.org/ resources/digest/0002enhancing.html

North Central Regional Educational Laboratory (NCREL). "Using Technology to Support Limited English-Proficient (LEP) Students' Learning Experiences." Available: http://www. ncrel.org/sdrs/areas/issues/methods/technlgy/ te900.htm

Note: These Professional Resources are listed for informational purposes. Scott Foresman does not necessarily agree with the opinions expressed in the various publications, Web sites, and sources. Information about online resources and availability is subject to change.

Index